JAN LOKPAL BILL

Indian Anti-Corruption Movement

JAN LOKPAL BILL

Indian Anti-Corruption Movement

Vijay Kumar Gupta
Dr Sudhir Dawra

MD PUBLICATIONS PVT LTD
NEW DELHI
www.mdppl.com

Published by :

MD Publications Pvt Ltd
"MD House", 11, Darya Ganj,
New Delhi-110 002
Phone : +91-11-45355555
E-mail : contact@mdppl.com
Website : www.mdppl.com

ISBN : 987-81-7533-361-1

Published and Printed by Mr. Pranav Gupta on behalf of
MD Publications Pvt Ltd at Printext, New Delhi.

Preface

The Jan Lokpal Bill is a draft of anti-corruption bill drawn up by prominent civil society activists seeking the appointment of a Jan Lokpal, an independent body that would investigate corruption cases, complete the investigation within a year and envisages trial in the case getting over in the next one year.

The Jan Lokpal Bill also referred to as the Citizens' Ombudsman Bill is a proposed independent anti-corruption law in India. Anti-corruption social activists proposed it as a more effective improvement to the original Lokpal bill, which is currently being proposed by the Government of India. The prefix "Jan" was added to signify the fact that these improvements include input provided by "ordinary citizens" through an activist-driven, non-governmental public consultation.

The Jan Lokpal Bill aims to effectively deter corruption, redress grievances of citizens and protect whistle-blowers. If made into law, the bill would create an independent Ombudsman body similar to the Election Commission of India called the Lokpal. It would be empowered to register and investigate complaints of corruption against politicians and bureaucrats without prior government approval. First introduced in 1968, the bill has failed to become law for over four decades.

The renewed calls for the bill arose over resentment of the major differences between the draft 2010 Lokpal Bill prepared by the government and that prepared by the members of the associated activists movement - N. Santosh Hegde, a former justice of the Supreme Court of India; Lokayukta of Karnataka;

Anna Hazare; Shanti Bhushan; Arvind Kejriwal; Kiran Bedi; Prashant Bhushan, a senior lawyer in the Supreme Court and members of the India against Corruption movement.

The bill's supporters consider existing laws too weak, full of contradictions and insufficiently empowered to combat corruption. On the other hand, critics of the Jan Lokpal Bill argue that the bill attempts to supersede existing constitutional bodies and attempts to create a super-institution with sweeping powers, which can be dangerous for the future of democracy.

We are very grateful to Mr. Pranav Gupta, Director of MD Publications Pvt Ltd, New Delhi, for his kind cooperation and support for this book.

Vijay Kumar Gupta
Dr Sudhir Dawra

Contents

1

JAN LOKPAL BILL

An Introduction

An act to create effective anti-corruption and grievance redressal systems at centre so that effective deterrent is created against corruption and to provide effective protection to whistleblowers.

1. Short title and commencement.

(1) This Act may be called the Anti-Corruption, Grievance Redressal and Whistleblower Protection Act, 2010.

(2) It shall come into force on the one hundred and twentieth day of its enactment.

2. Definitions. In this Act, unless the context otherwise requires;

(1) "Action" means any action taken by a public servant in the discharge of his functions as such public servant and includes decision, recommendation or finding or in any other manner and includes willful failure or omission to act and all other expressions relating to such action shall be construed accordingly;

(2) "Allegation" in relation to a public servant includes any affirmation that such public servant;

(a) has indulged in misconduct, if he is a government servant;

(b) has indulged in corruption

(3) "complaint" includes any grievance or allegation or a request by whistleblower for protection and appropriate action.

(4) "corruption" includes anything made punishable under Chapter IX of the Indian Penal Code or under the Prevention of Corruption Act, 1988;

Provided that if any person obtains any benefit from the government by violating any laws or rules, that person along with the public servants who directly or indirectly helped that person obtain those benefits, shall be deemed to have indulged in corruption.

(5) "Government" or "Central Government" means Government of India.

(6) "Government Servant" means any person who is or was any time appointed to a civil service or post in connection with the affairs of the Central Government or High Courts or Supreme Court either on deputation or permanent or temporary or on contractual employment but would not include the judges.

(7) "grievance" means a claim by a person that he sustained injustice or undue hardship in consequence of mal-administration;

(8) "Lokpal" means;

a. Benches constituted under this Act and performing their functions as laid down under various provisions of this Act; or

b. Any officer or employee, exercising its powers and carrying out its functions and responsibilities, in the manner and to the extent, assigned to it under this Act, or under various rules, regulations or orders made under various provisions of this Act.

c. For all other purposes, the Chairperson and members acting collectively as a body;

(9) "Mal-administration" means action taken or purporting to have been taken in the exercise of administrative function in any case where,-

a. such action or the administrative procedure or practice governing such action is unreasonable, unjust, oppressive or improperly discriminatory; or

b. there has been willful negligence or undue delay in taking such action or the administrative procedure or practice governing such action involves undue delay;

(10) "Misconduct" means misconduct as defined in CCS Conduct Rules and which has vigilance angle.

(11) "public authority" means any authority or body or institution of self- government established or constituted;

a. by or under the Constitution;

b. by any other law made by Parliament;

c. by notification issued or order made by the Government, and includes any body owned, controlled or substantially financed by the Government;

(12) "Public servant" means a person who is or was at any time,-

(a) the Prime Minister;

(b) a Minister;

(c) a Member of Parliament;

(d) Judges of High Courts and Supreme Court;

(e) a Government servant;

(f) the Chairman or Vice-Chairman (by whatever name called) or a member of a local authority in the control of the Central Government or a statutory body or corporation established by or under any law of the Parliament of India, including a co-operative society, or a Government Company within the meaning of section 617 of the Companies Act, 1956 and members of any Committee or Board, statutory or non-statutory, constituted by the Government;

(g) Such other authorities as the Central Government may, by notification, from time to time, specify;

(13) "Vigilance angle" includes;

(a) All acts of corruption

(b) Gross or willful negligence; recklessness in decision making; blatant violations of systems and procedures; exercise of discretion in excess, where no ostensible/public interest is evident; failure to keep the controlling authority/superiors informed in time.

(c) Failure/delay in taking action, if under law the government servant ought to do so, against subordinates on complaints of corruption or dereliction of duties or abuse of office by the subordinates.

(d) Indulging in discrimination through one's conduct, directly or indirectly.

(e) Victimizing Whistle Blowers.

(f) Any undue/unjustified delay in the disposal of a case, perceived after considering all relevant factors, would reinforce a conclusion as to the presence of vigilance angle in a case.

(g) Make unfair investigation or enquiry to either unduly help culprits or fabricate the innocent.

(h) Any other matter as notified from time to time by Lokpal.

(14) "Whistleblower" is any person who faces threat of (1) professional harm, including but not limited to illegitimate transfers, denial of promotions, denial of appropriate perks, departmental proceedings, discrimination or (2) physical harm or (3) is actually subjected to such harm; because of either making a complaint to Lokpal under this Act or for filing an application under Right to Information Act.

3. Establishment of the institution of Lokpal and appointment of Lokpal.

(1) There shall be an institution known as Lokpal which shall consist of one Chairperson and ten members along with its officers and employees. The Lokpal shall be headed by its Chairperson.

(2) The Chairperson and members of Lokpal shall be selected in such manner as laid down in this Act.

(3) A person appointed as Chairperson or member of Lokpal shall, before entering upon his office, make and subscribe before the President, an oath or affirmation in the form as prescribed.

(4) The Government shall appoint the Chairperson and members of the first Lokpal and set up the institution with all its logistics and assets within six months of enactment of this Act.

(5) The Government shall fill up a vacancy of the Chairperson or a member caused due to: a) Retirement, 3 months before the member or the Chairperson retires. b) Any other unforeseen reason, within a month of such vacancy.

CHAIRPERSON AND MEMBERS OF LOKPAL

4. The Chairperson and members of Lokpal not to have held certain offices. The Chairperson and members of Lokpal shall not be serving or former member of either the Parliament or the Legislature of any State and shall not hold any office or trust of profit (other than the office as Chairperson or member) or would have ever been connected with any political party or carry on any business or practice any profession and accordingly, before he enters upon his office, a person appointed as the Chairperson or member of Lokpal shall-

(i) if he holds any office of trust or profit, resign from such office; or

(ii) if he is carrying on any business, sever his connection with the conduct and management of such business; or

(iii) if he is practicing any profession, suspend practice of such profession.

(iv) If he is associated directly or indirectly with any other activity, which is likely cause conflict of interest in the performance of his duties in Lokpal, he should suspend his association with that activity.

Provided that if even after the suspension, the earlier association of that person with such activity is likely to adversely affect his performance at Lokpal, that person shall not be appointed as a member or Chairperson of Lokpal.

5. Term of office and other conditions of service of Lokpal.

(1) A person appointed as the Chairperson or member of Lokpal shall hold office for a term of five years from the date on which he enters upon his office;

Provided further that.-

(a) The Chairperson or member of Lokpal may, by writing under his hand addressed to the President, resign his office;

(b) The Chairperson or member may be removed from office in the manner provided in this Act.

(2) There shall be paid to the Chairperson and each member every month a salary equal to that of the Chief Justice of India and that of the judge of the Supreme Court respectively;

(3) The allowances and pension payable to and other conditions of service of the Chairperson or a member shall be such as may be prescribed;

Provided that the allowances and pension payable to and other conditions of service of the Chairperson or members shall not be varied to his disadvantage after his appointment.

(4) The administrative expenses of the office of the Lokpal including all salaries, allowances and pensions payable to or in respect of persons serving in that office, shall be charged on the Consolidated Fund of India.

(5) There shall be a separate fund by the name of "Lokpal fund" in which penalties/fines imposed by the Lokpal shall be deposited and in which 10% of the loss of Public Money detected/ prevented on account of investigations by Lokpal shall also be deposited by the Government. Disposal of such fund shall be completely at the discretion of the Lokpal and such fund shall be used only for enhancement/upgradation/ extension of the infrastructure of Lokpal.

(6) The Chairperson or members shall not be eligible for appointment on any position in Government of India or Government of any state or for fighting elections, if he has ever held the position of the Chairperson or a member for any period.

Provided however that a member or Chairperson may be reappointed for one more term or a member may be appointed as the Chairperson, however, that any person shall not serve for more than a total of two terms.

6. Appointment of the Chairperson and members.

1. The Chairperson and members shall be appointed by the President on the recommendation of a selection committee.
2. Following persons shall not be eligible to become Chairman or Member in Lokpal:
   (a) Any person who was ever chargesheeted for any offence under IPC or PC Act or was ever penalized under CCS Conduct Rules.
   (b) Any person who is less than 40 years in age.
3. At least four members of Lokpal shall have legal background.
4. The members and Chairperson should have unimpeachable integrity and should have demonstrated their resolve and efforts to fight against corruption in the past.
5. A selection committee consisting of the following shall be set up:
   a. The Chairpersons of both Houses of Parliament
   b. Two senior most judges of Supreme Court
   c. Two senior most Chief Justices of High Courts.
   d. All Nobel Laureates of Indian Origin
   e. Chairperson of National Human Rights Commission
   f. Last two Magsaysay Award winners of Indian origin
   g. Comptroller and Auditor General of India
   h. Chief Election Commissioner
   i. Bharat Ratna Award winners

j. After the first set of selection process, the outgoing members and Chairperson of Lokpal.

6. The senior most judge of Supreme Court shall act as the Chairperson of the selection committee.

7. The following selection process shall be followed:

   a. Recommendations shall be invited through open advertisements in prescribed format.

   b. Each person recommending shall be expected to justify the selection of his candidate giving examples from the past achievements of the candidate.

   c. The list of candidates along with their recommendations received in the format mentioned above shall be displayed on a website.

   d. Each member of the selection committee, on the basis of the above material, shall recommend such number of names as there are vacancies.

   e. A priority list shall be prepared with the candidate receiving recommendations from maximum number of members of selection committee at the top. The candidates recommended by same number of members shall be treated at par.

   f. This priority list shall be displayed on the website.

   g. Around three times the names as there are vacancies, shall be shortlisted from the top.

   h. Public feedback shall be invited on the shortlisted names by putting these names on the website.

   i. The selection committee may decide to use any means to collect more information about the background and past achievements of the shortlisted candidates.

j. Selection committee shall invite shortlisted candidates for discussions, video recordings of which shall be made public.

k. All the material obtained so far about the candidates shall be made available to each member of the selection committee in advance. The members shall make their own assessment of each candidate.

l. The selection committee shall meet and discuss the material so received about each candidate. The final selections for the Chairperson and members shall be made preferably through consensus.

Provided that if three or more members, for reasons to be recorded in writing, object to the selection of any member, he shall not be selected.

m. All meetings of selection committee shall be video recorded and shall be made public.

8. The Prime Minister shall recommend the names finalized by the selection committee to the President immediately, who shall order such appointments within a month of receipt of the same.

9. If any of the members of the selection committee retires while a selection process is going on, that member will continue on the selection committee till the end of that process.

7. Removal of Chairperson or members.

(1) The Chairperson or any member shall not be removed from his office except by an order of the President.

(2) They can be removed on one or more of the following grounds:

a. Proved misbehavior.

b. Professional or physical incapacity.

c. If he is adjudged to be insolvent.

d. Has been charged of an offence which involves moral turpitude.

e. If he engages during his term of office in any paid employment outside the duties of his office.

f. Has acquired such financial interests or other interests which are likely to affect prejudicially his functions as member or Chairperson.

g. If he is guided by considerations extraneous to the merits of the case either to favor someone or to implicate someone through any act of omission or commission.

h. If any member or Chairperson tries to or actually unduly influences any government functionary.

i. If he commits any act of omission or commission which is punishable under Prevention of Corruption Act or is a misconduct.

j. If a member or the Chairperson in any way, concerned or interested in any contract or agreement made by or on behalf of the Government of India or participates in any way in the profit thereof or in any benefit or emolument arising there from otherwise than as a member and in common with the other members of an incorporated company, he shall be deemed to be guilty of misbehavior.

(3) The following process shall be followed for the removal of any member or Chairperson:

(a) Any person may move an application/

petition before the Supreme Court seeking removal of one or more of the members of Chairperson of Lokpal alleging one or more of the grounds for removal and providing evidence for the same.

(b) Supreme Court will hear the matter by a bench of three or more Judges on receipt of such petition and may take one or more of the following steps:

(i) order an investigation to be done by a Special Investigation Team appointed by the Supreme Court if a prima facie case is made out and if the matter cannot be judged based on affidavits of the parties. The Special Investigation Team shall submit its report within three months.

(ii) Pending investigations under sub-clause (i) by Special Investigation Team, the Supreme Court may decide to order withdrawal of part or complete work from that member.

(iii) dismiss the petition if no case is made out.

(iv) if the grounds are proved, recommend to the President for removal of the said member or Chairperson

(v) direct registration and investigation of cases with appropriate agencies if there is prima facie case of commission of an offence punishable under Prevention of Corruption Act.

(c) The three judge bench shall be constituted by a panel of five senior most judges of the Supreme Court.

Provided that if there are any proceedings going on against any judge in Lokpal, he shall not be a part of either the panel or the bench.

(d) The Supreme Court shall not dismiss such petitions in liminae.

(e) If the Supreme Court concludes that the petition has been made with mischievous or malafide motives, the Court may order imposition of fine or imprisonment upto one year against the complainant.

(f) On receipt of a recommendation from the Supreme Court under this section, the Prime Minister shall recommend it to the President immediately and the President shall order removal of said members within a month of receipt of the same.

POWERS AND FUNCTIONS OF LOKPAL

8. Functions of Lokpal.

(1) Lokpal shall be responsible for receiving:

  (a) Complaints where there are allegations of such acts of omission or commission which are punishable under Prevention of Corruption Act

  (b) Complaints where there are allegations of misconduct by a government servant

  (c) Grievances

  (d) Complaints from whistleblowers

(2) Lokpal, after getting such enquiries and investigations done as it deems fit, may take one or more of the following actions:

  a. Close the case if prima facie, the complaint is not made out or

  b. Initiate prosecution against public servants as well as those private entities which are party to the act

c. Order imposition of appropriate penalties under CCS Conduct Rules

Provided that if an officer is finally convicted under Prevention of Corruption Act, major penalty of dismissal shall be imposed on such government servant.

d. Order cancellation or modification of a license or lease or permission or contract or agreement, which was the subject matter of investigation.

e. Blacklist the concerned firm or company or contractor or any other entity involved in that act of corruption.

f. Issue appropriate directions to appropriate authorities for redressal of grievance in such time and in such manner as is specified in the order.

g. Invoke its powers under this Act if its orders are not duly complied with and ensure due compliance of its orders.

h. Take necessary action to provide protection to a whistleblower as per various provisions of this Act.

(3) Suo moto initiate appropriate action under this Act if any case, of the nature mentioned in clauses (1), (2), (3) or (4), comes to the knowledge of the Lokpal from any source.

(4) Issue such directions, as are necessary, from time to time, to appropriate authorities so as to make such changes in their work practices, administration or other systems so as to reduce the scope and possibility for corruption, misconduct and public grievances.

(5) Lokpal shall be deemed to be "Disciplinary authority" or "appointing authority" for the

purpose of imposing penalties under CCS Conduct Rules.

(6) Section 19 of Prevention of Corruption Act shall be deleted.

(7) Section 197 of CRPC shall not apply to any proceedings under this Act. All permissions, which need to be sought for initiating investigations or for initiating prosecutions under any Act shall be deemed to have been granted once Lokpal grants such permissions.

9. Issue of Search Warrant, etc.

(1) Where, in consequence of information in his possession, the Lokpal

(a) has reason to believe that any person;

(i) to whom a summon or notice under this Act, has, been or might be issued, will not or would not produce or cause to be produced any property, document or thing which will be necessary or useful for or relevant to any inquiry or other proceeding to be conducted by him;

(ii) is in possession of any money, bullion, jewellery or other valuable article or thing and such money, bullion, jewellery or other valuable article or thing represents either wholly or partly income or property which has not been disclosed to the authorities for the purpose of any law or rule in force which requires such disclosure to be made; or

(b) considers that the purposes of any inquiry or other proceedings to be conducted by him will be served by a general search or inspection, he may by a search warrant authorize any Police officer not below the rank of an Inspector of Police to conduct a search or carry out an inspection in accordance therewith and in particular to, -

(i) enter and search any building or place where he has reason to suspect that such property, document, money, bullion, jewellery or other valuable article or thing is kept;

(ii) search any person who is reasonably suspected of concealing about his person any article for which search should be made;

(iii) break open the lock of any door, box, locker safe, almirah or other receptacle for exercising the powers conferred by sub-clause (i) where the keys thereof are not available.

Seize any such property, document, money, bullion, jewellery or other valuable article or thing found as a result of such search;

(iv) place marks of identification on any property or document or make or cause to be made; extracts or copies there from; or

(v) make a note or an inventory of any such property, document, money, bullion, Jewellery or other valuable article or thing.

(2) The provisions of the Code of Criminal Procedure, 1973, relating to search and seizure shall apply, so far as may be, to searches and seizures under sub-section (1).

(3) A warrant issued under sub-section (1) shall for all purposes, be deemed to be a warrant issued by a court under section 93 of the Code of

Criminal Procedure, 1973.

10. Evidence.

(1) Subject to the provisions of this section, for the purpose of any investigation (including the preliminary inquiry, if any, before such investigation) under this Act, the Lokpal may require any public servant or any other person who, in his opinion is able to furnish information or produce documents relevant to the investigation, to furnish any such information or produce any such document.

(2) For the purpose of any such investigation (including the preliminary inquiry) the Lokpal shall have all the powers of a civil court while trying a suit under the Code of Civil Procedure, 1908 , in respect of the following matters, namely:-

- (a) Summoning and enforcing the attendance of any person and examining him on oath;
- (b) Requiring the discovery and production of any document;
- (c) Receiving evidence on affidavits;
- (d) Requisitioning any public record or copy thereof from any court or office;
- (e) Issuing commissions for the examination of witnesses or documents;
- (f) Ordering payment of compensatory cost in respect of a false or vexatious claim or defence;
- (g) ordering cost for causing delay;
- (h) Such other matters as may be prescribed.

(3) Any proceeding before the Lokpal shall be deemed to be a judicial proceeding with in the meaning of section 193 of the Indian Penal Code.

11. Reports of Lokpal, etc.

(1) The Chairperson of Lokpal shall present annually

a consolidated report in prescribed format on its performance to the President.

(2) On receipt of the annual report, the President shall cause a copy thereof together with an explanatory memorandum to be laid before each House of the Parliament.

(3) The Lokpal shall publish every month on its website the list of cases disposed with brief details of each such case, outcome and action taken or proposed to be taken in that case. It shall also publish lists of all cases received by the Lokpal during the previous month, cases disposed and cases which are pending.

12. Lokpal to be a deemed police officer.

(1) For the purposes of section 36 of Criminal Procedure Code, the Chairperson, members of Lokpal and the officers in investigation wing of Lokpal shall be deemed to be police officers.

(2) While investigating any offence under Prevention of Corruption Act 1988, they shall be competent to investigate any offence under any other law in the same case.

13. Powers in case of non-compliance of orders.

(1) Each order of Lokpal shall clearly specify the names of the officials who are required to execute that order, the manner in which it should be executed and the time period within which that order should be complied with.

(2) If the order is not complied with within the time or in the manner directed, Lokpal may decide to impose a fine on the officials responsible for the non-compliance of its orders.

(3) The Drawing and Disbursing Officer of that Department shall be directed to deduct such amount of fine as is clearly specified by the Lokpal in its order made in sub-section (2) from the salaries of the officers specified in the order.

Provided that no penalty shall be imposed without giving a reasonable opportunity of being heard.

Provided that if the Drawing and Disbursing Officer fails to deduct the salary as specified in the said order, he shall make himself liable for a similar penalty.

(4) In order to get its orders complied with, the Lokpal shall have, and exercise the same jurisdiction powers and authority in respect of contempt of itself as a High court has and may exercise, and, for this purpose, the provisions of the Contempt of Courts Act, 1971 (Central Act 70 of 1971) shall have the effect subject to the modification that the references therein to the High Court shall be construed as including a reference to the Lokpal.

13A. Special Judges under section 4 of Prevention of Corruption Act. On an annual basis, Lokpal shall make an assessment of the number of Special Judges required under section 4 of Prevention of Corruption Act 1988 in each area and the Government shall appoint such number of Judges within three months of receipt of such recommendation.

Provided that Lokpal shall recommend such number of Special Judges so that trial in each case under this Act is completed within a year.

13B. Issue of Letter Rogatory. A bench of Lokpal shall have powers to issue Letters Rogatory in any case pending with Lokpal.

FUNCTIONING OF LOKPAL

14. Functioning of Lokpal.

(1) The Chairperson shall be responsible for overall administration and supervision of the institution of Lokpal.

(2) All policy level decisions including formulation of regulations, developing internal systems for

the functioning of Lokpal, assigning functions to various officials in Lokpal, delegation of powers to various functionaries in Lokpal etc shall be taken by the Chairperson and the members collectively as a body.

(3) The Chairperson shall have an annual meeting with the Prime Minister to assess the needs of Lokpal for finances and manpower. Lokpal shall be provided resources by the Government on the basis of outcome of this meeting.

(4) Lokpal shall function in benches of three or more members. Benches shall be constituted randomly and cases shall be assigned to them randomly by computer. Each bench shall consist of at least one member with legal background.

(5) Such benches shall be responsible for

(i) granting permission to close any case after a preliminary enquiry

(ii) granting permission to either close a case after investigations or issuing orders imposing penalties under CCS Conduct Rules and/or for initiating prosecution in that case.

(iii) Issuing orders under section 28 and section 13B.

(6) Lokpal may decide to initiate investigations into any case suo moto also.

(7) The decision to initiate investigation or prosecution against any member of the Cabinet or any judge of High Court or Supreme Court shall be taken in a meeting of all the existing members and the Chairperson. Minutes and records of such meetings shall be made public.

15. Making a complaint to the Lokpal.

(1) Subject to the provisions of this Act, any person may make a complaint under this Act to the Lokpal.

Provided that in case of a grievance, if the person aggrieved is dead or for any reason, unable to act for himself, the complaint may be made or if it is already made may be continued by his legal representatives or by any other person who is authorized by him in writing in this behalf.

(2) A complaint could be on a plain paper but should contain all such details as prescribed by Lokpal.

(3) On receipt of a complaint, the Lokpal shall decide whether it is an allegation or a grievance or a request for whistleblower protection or a mixture of two or more of these.

(4) Every complaint shall have to be compulsorily disposed off by the Lokpal.

Provided that no complaint, other than those which are anonymous or pseudonymous, shall be closed without hearing the complainant.

16. Matters which may be investigated by the Lokpal. Subject to the provisions of this Act, the Lokpal may investigate any action which is taken by or with the general or specific approval of a public servant where a complaint involving a grievance or an allegation is made in respect of such action.

Provided that the Lokpal may also investigate such action suo moto or if it is referred to it by the government, if such action can be or could have been in his recorded opinion, subject of a grievance or an allegation.

17. Matters not subject to investigation.

(1) The Lokpal shall not conduct any investigation under this Act in case of a grievance in respect of any action-

(i) If the complainant has or had, any remedy by way of appeal, revision, review or any other remedy before any other authority provided in any other law and he has not availed of the same.

(ii) Taken by a judicial or quasi-judicial body, unless the complainant alleges malafides

(iii) If the substance of the entire grievance is pending before any court or quasi-judicial body of competent jurisdiction.

(iv) any grievance where there is inordinate and inexplicable delay.

(2) Nothing in this Act shall be construed as authorising the Lokpal to investigate any action which is taken by or with the approval of the Presiding Officer of either House of Parliament.

(3) The provisions of this Act shall be in addition to the provisions of any other enactment or any rule or law under which any remedy by way of appeal, revision, review or in any other manner is available to a person making a complaint under this Act in respect of any action and nothing in this Act shall limit or affect the right of such person to avail of such remedy.

(4) Nothing in this section shall bar Lokpal from entertaining a complaint making an allegation of misconduct or corruption or a complaint from a whistleblower seeking protection.

18. Provisions relating to complaints and investigations.

(i) (a) The Lokpal, on receipt of a complaint in the nature of an allegation or a grievance or a combination of the two, or in a case initiated on his own motion, may on perusing the documents, either decide to proceed to enquire or investigate into that complaint or decide, to make such preliminary inquiry before proceeding to enquire or investigate into such complaint or direct any other person to make such preliminary inquiry as it deems fit for ascertaining whether there exists reasonable ground for conducting the investigation. The outcome of such preliminary enquiry, and if the complaint is being closed along with reasons for the same and all material collected during preliminary enquiry, shall be communicated to the complainant.

Provided that if any case is closed, all documents related thereto shall thereafter be treated as public. Every month, a list of all such cases shall be put on the website with reasons for closing a case. All material connected with such closed cases will be provided to anyone seeking it under Right to Information Act.

Provided further that if the complaint contains verifiable and specific information about misconduct or corruption, then that case shall not be rejected even if the complaint is anonymous.

Provided further that no complaint of allegation shall be rejected by questioning the motives or intention of the complainant.

Provided further that all hearings before Lokpal shall be video recorded and shall be available to any member of the public on payment of copying costs.

(b) The procedure for preliminary enquiry of a complaint shall be such as the Lokpal deems appropriate in the circumstances of the case and in particular, the Lokpal may, if it deems necessary to do so, call for the comments of the public servant concerned.

Provided that the preliminary enquiry should be completed and a decision taken whether to close a case or to proceed with investigations within one month of receipt of any complaint.

(ii) Where the Lokpal proposes, either directly or after making preliminary inquiry, to conduct any investigation under this Act, he.-

(a) may make such order as to the safe custody

of documents relevant to the investigation, as it deems fit.

(b) at appropriate stage of investigations or in the end, it shall forward a copy of the complaint, its findings and copy of the material relied upon to the concerned public servant and the complainant,

(c) shall afford to such public servant and the complainant an opportunity to offer comments and be heard.

Provided that such hearing shall be held in public, except in such rare circumstances, to be recorded in writing, will it be held in camera.

(iii) The conduct of an investigation under this Act against a Public servant in respect of any action shall not affect such action, or any power or duty of any other public servant to take further action with respect to any matter subject to the investigation.

(iv) If, during the course of preliminary inquiry or investigation under this Act, the Lokpal is prima facie satisfied that the allegation or grievance in respect of any action is likely to be sustained either wholly or partly, he may, through an interim order, direct the public servant concerned to stay the implementation or enforcement of the decision or action complained against, or to take such mandatory or preventive action, on such terms and conditions, as he may specify in his order to prevent further harm from taking place.

(v) The Lokpal, either during the course of investigations, if it is satisfied that prosecution is likely to be initiated in that case, or at the end of the investigations at the time of initiating prosecution, shall make a list of moveable and immoveable assets of all the accused in that case and shall notify the same. No transfer of the same shall be permitted after such notification. In the event of final conviction, the court shall be empowered to recover loss determined under section 19 of this Act from this property, in addition to other measures.

(vi) If during the course of investigation or enquiry into a complaint, Lokpal feels that continuance of a public servant in that position could adversely affect the course of investigations or enquiry or that the said person is likely to impact evidence or witnesses, the Lokpal may issue appropriate orders including transfer of that public servant from that position or his suspension.

Provided that such orders shall not be passed against the Prime Minister.

(vii) In case of a grievance, the Lokpal may issue interim orders to the appropriate authority recommending grant of interim relief to the complainant if he is satisfied at any stage of preliminary inquiry on investigation that the complainant has sustained injustice or undue hardship in consequence of any decision or action of a public servant.

(viii) The Lokpal may, at any stage of inquiry or investigation under this Act, direct through an interim order, appropriate authorities to take such action as is necessary, including suspension of a government servant, pending inquiry or investigation.-

(i) to safeguard wastage or damage of public property or public revenue by the administrative acts of the public servant;

(ii) to prevent further acts of misconduct by the public servant;

(iii) to prevent the public servant from secreting the assets allegedly acquired by him by corrupt means;

(ix) Where after investigation into a complaint, the Lokpal is satisfied that the complaint involving an allegation against the public servant is substantiated and that the public servant concerned should not continue to hold the post held by him, the Lokpal shall pass orders to that effect. In case of public servant being a Minister, Lokpal shall make such recommendation to the President, who shall decide either to accept such recommendation or reject it within a month of its receipt.

Provided that the provisions of this section shall not apply to the Prime Minister.

(x) If, after enquiry into a grievance and after affording reasonable opportunity of being heard to both the complainant and the public authority, the Lokpal is satisfied that such grievance is substantiated either wholly or partly, he shall,

i. Pass appropriate orders directing appropriate authorities to redress the grievance in a manner and within the time prescribed in the order, and

ii. Direct the appropriate authorities to deduct from the salary of the officials mentioned in the order, such penalty amounts as are directed by Lokpal, which shall not be less than Rs 250 per day of delay calculated from day the time limit mentioned in citizens' charter for redressing that grievance got over, and

iii. Direct the appropriate authorities to compensate the complainant with such amounts as mentioned in the order.

Provided that any grievance shall be disposed within 15 days of its receipt.

Provided further that if it relates to life and liberty of a person or if the matter is such as to warrant immediate attention and the Lokpal is so satisfied, the same shall be disposed within 48 hours.

(xi) All records and information of Lokpal shall be public and shall be provided under Right to Information Act, even at the stage of investigation or enquiry, unless release of such information would adversely affect the process of enquiry or investigation.

Provided that no information in any case shall be withheld under Right to Information Act after the completion of enquiry or investigation.

RECOVERY OF LOSS TO THE GOVERNMENT AND PUNISHMENTS

19. Recovery of loss to the Government. If a person is convicted of an offence under Prevention of Corruption Act, then the trial court will also quantify the loss caused to the government and apportion that amount to various convicts from whom this money must be recovered as arrears of land revenue.

19A. Punishments for offences. For offences mentioned in Chapter III of Prevention of Corruption Act, punishment shall not be less than five years which may extend upto life imprisonment.

Provided that if the accused is any officer of the rank of Joint Secretary in the state or above or a Minister, the punishment shall not be less than ten years.

Provided further that if the offence is of the nature mentioned in proviso to section 2(4) of this Act and if the beneficiary is any corporate house, in addition to other punishments mentioned in this Act and under Prevention of Corruption Act, a fine amounting to five times the loss caused to the government shall be recovered from the accused and the recovery may be done from the assets of the company and from the personal assets of all Directors of the company, if the assets of the accused are inadequate.

WHISTLEBLOWER PROTECTION

20. Protection of Whistleblower.

(1) A whistleblower may write to Lokpal seeking protection from threat of physical or professional victimization or if he has been subjected to such professional or physical victimization.

(2) On receiving such a complaint, Lokpal shall take following steps:

(a) Threat of professional victimization: Lokpal shall conduct appropriate enquiries and if it feels that there is a real threat to the person and the threat is on account of that person having made an allegation under this Act, then the Lokpal shall pass appropriate orders, as soon as possible but in not more than a month of receipt of such complaint, directing appropriate authorities to take such steps as directed by the Lokpal.

(b) If a person complains that he has already been victimized professionally on account of making an allegation under this Act, Lokpal shall, after conducting enquiries, if he is of the opinion that the victimization is indeed because of that person's having made an allegation under this Act, pass appropriate orders, as soon as possible but in not more than a month, directing appropriate authorities to take such steps as directed by the Lokpal.

Provided that for clause (a) Lokpal may, but for clause (b) the Lokpal shall, also issue orders imposing penalties under CCS Conduct Rules against the officer or officials who issued threats or caused victimization.

Provided further that no such penalties shall be imposed without giving an opportunity of being heard to the affected officials.

(c) Threat of physical victimization: Lokpal shall conduct appropriate enquiries and if it feels that there is a real threat to the person and the threat is on account of that person having made an allegation under this Act or for having filed an RTI application to any public authority covered under this Act, then notwithstanding anything contained in any other law, the Lokpal shall pass appropriate orders, as soon as possible but in not more than a week, directing appropriate authorities, including police, to take such steps as directed by the Lokpal to provide adequate security to that person, to register criminal cases against those who are issuing threats and also to take all such steps necessary to mitigate circumstances leading to such threat.

Provided that if the threat is imminent, Lokpal may decide to act immediately, within a few hours to prevent physical assault on that person.

(d) If a person complains that he has already been physically assaulted on account of making an allegation under this Act and if Lokpal is satisfied after conducting enquiries that the person has been assaulted because of his having made an allegation under this Act or for filing an RTI application in any of the public authorities covered under this Act, then notwithstanding anything else contained in any other law, the Lokpal shall pass such orders, as soon as possible but in not more than 24 hours, directing the concerned authorities to take such steps as directed by the Lokpal to provide adequate security to that person, to register criminal cases and also to ensure that no further harm visits on that person.

(e) If the whistleblower has alleged an act punishable under Prevention of Corruption Act, then for cases under clause (c), Lokpal may and for cases under clause (d), the Lokpal shall, assign the allegations made by that person to a special team, put it on a fast track and complete investigations in that case in not more than a month.

(f) If the whistleblower has alleged an act punishable under any law other than the Prevention of Corruption Act, then for cases under clause (c), Lokpal may and for cases under clause (d), the Lokpal shall, direct the agency which has the powers to enforce that law to assign the allegations made by the whistleblower to a special team, put it on a fast track and complete investigations in that case in such time as directed by the Lokpal.

(g) Lokpal shall have the powers to issue directions to appropriate agencies in the cases covered under clause (f), monitor such investigations and if necessary, issue directions to that agency to do the investigations in the manner as directed by the Lokpal.

(3) If any complainant requests that his identity should be kept secret, Lokpal shall ensure the same. Lokpal shall prescribe detailed procedures on how such complainants shall be dealt with.

(4) Lokpal shall Issue orders to the Public Authorities to make necessary changes in their policies and practices to prevent recurrence of victimization.

GRIEVANCE REDRESSAL SYSTEMS

21. Citizens' Charters.

(1) Each public authority shall be responsible for ensuring the preparation and implementation of Citizens Charter, within a reasonable time, and not exceeding one year from the coming into force of this Act.

(2) Every Citizens Charter shall enumerate the commitments of the respective public authority to the citizens, officer responsible for meeting each such commitment and the time limit with in which the commitment shall be met.

(3) Each public authority shall designate an official called Public Grievance Redressal Officer, whom a complainant should approach for any violation of the Citizens Charter.

(4) Every public authority shall review and revise its Citizens Charter at least once every year through a process of public consultation.

(5) Lokpal may direct any public authority to make such changes in their citizens' charter as are mentioned in that order.

(6) No grievance shall be accepted by Lokpal if 15 days have not elapsed after submission of complaint by the complainant with the Public Grievance redressal Officer of that Public Authority.

Provided that if Lokpal feels that considering the gravity or urgency of the grievance, it is necessary to do so, the Lokpal may decide to accept such grievance earlier also.

EMPLOYEES, STAFF AND AUTHORITIES IN LOKPAL

22. Chief Vigilance Officer.

(1) There shall be a Chief Vigilance Officer in each public authority to be selected and appointed by Lokpal.

(2) He shall not be from the same public authority.

(3) He shall be a person of impeccable integrity and ability to take proactive measures against corruption.

(4) He shall be responsible for accepting complaints against any public authority and shall transfer the complaints related to other public authorities within two days of receipt.

(5) He shall be responsible for carrying out all such responsibilities as assigned to him from time to time by Lokpal including dealing with complaints in the manner as laid down by Lokpal from time to time. Provided that the complaints which require investigations under Prevention of Corruption Act 1988 shall be transferred to the Investigative wing of Lokpal.

Provided further that the complaints, other than grievances, against officers of the level of Joint

Secretary or above shall not be dealt by the Chief Vigilance Officer and shall be transferred to the Lokpal, who shall set up a committee of Chief Vigilance Officers of three other public authorities to enquire into such complaint.

(6) All the grievances shall be received and disposed by Chief Vigilance Officer on behalf of Lokpal, if the citizen fails to get satisfactory redressal from Public Grievance Officer under section 21 of this Act.

23. Staff of Lokpal, etc.

(1) There shall be such officers and employees as may be prescribed to assist the Lokpal in the discharge of their functions under this Act.

(2) The number and categories of officers and employees shall be decided by the Lokpal in consultation with the government.

(3) The categories, recruitment and conditions of service of the officers and employees referred in sub-section (1) including such special conditions or special pay as may be necessary for enabling them to act without fear in the discharge of their functions, shall be such as may be prescribed according to the recommendations of Lokpal.

Provided that no official, whose integrity is in doubt, shall be considered for being posted in Lokpal.

Provided further that all officers and employees, who work in Lokpal on deputation or otherwise shall be eligible for the same terms and conditions as prescribed under this clause.

(4) Without prejudice to the provisions of sub-section (1), the Lokpal may for the purpose of conducting investigations under this Act utilize the services of.-

(a) any officer or investigating agency of the Central Government; or

(b) any officer or investigating agency of any other Government with the prior concurrence of that Government; or

(c) any person or any other agency.

(5) The officers and other employees referred to in sub-section (1) shall be under the administrative and disciplinary control of the Lokpal:

(6) Lokpal shall have the powers to choose its own officials. Lokpal may enlist officials on deputation from other government agencies for a fixed tenure or it may enlist officials on permanent basis from other government agencies or it may appoint people from outside on permanent basis or on a fixed tenure basis.

(7) The staff and officers shall be entitled to such pay scales and other allowances, which may be different and more than the ordinary pay scales in the Central Government, as are decided by the Lokpal from time to time, in consultation with the Prime Minister, so as to attract honest and efficient people to work in Lokpal.

24. Repeal and savings.

(1) The Central Vigilance Commission Act shall stand repealed.

(2) Notwithstanding such repeal, any act or thing done under the said Act shall be deemed to have been done under this Act and may be continued and completed under the corresponding provisions of this Act.

(3) All enquiries and investigations and other disciplinary proceedings pending before the Central Vigilance Commission and which have not been disposed of, shall stand transferred to and be continued by the Lokpal as if they were commenced before him under this Act.

(4) Notwithstanding anything contained in any Act, the posts of the Secretary and other Officers and Employees of the Central Vigilance Commission are hereby abolished and they are hereby appointed as the Secretary and other officers and employees of the Lokpal. The salaries, allowances and other terms and conditions of services of the said Secretary, officers and other employees shall, until they are varied, be the same as to which they were entitled to immediately before the commencement of this Act.

(5) All vigilance administration under the control of all Departments of Central Government, Ministries of the Central Government, corporations established by or under any Central Act, Government companies, societies and local authorities owned or controlled by the Central Government shall stand transferred, along with its personnel, assets and liabilities to Lokpal for all purposes.

(6) The personnel working in vigilance wings of the agencies mentioned in sub-section (5) shall be deemed to be on deputation to Lokpal for a period of five years from the date they are transferred to Lokpal. However, Lokpal may decide to repatriate any one of them anytime.

(7) That Department from where any personnel have been transferred to Lokpal under sub-section (5), shall cease to have any control over the administration and functions of transferred personnel.

(8) Lokpal shall rotate the personnel and create vigilance wing of each department in such a way that no personnel from the same department get posted for vigilance functions in the same department.

(9) No person shall be employed with Lokpal against whom any vigilance enquiry or any criminal case is pending at the time of being considered.

25. Investigation Wing of Lokpal.

(1) There shall be an investigation wing at Lokpal.

(2) Notwithstanding anything contained in section 17 of Prevention of Corruption Act, such officers of Investigation wing, upto the level as decided by Lokpal, shall have, in relation to the investigation and arrest of persons throughout India, in connection with investigation of complaints under this Act, all the powers, duties, privileges and liabilities which members of Delhi Special Police Establishment have in connection with the investigation of offences committed therein.

(3) That part of Delhi Special Police Establishment, in so far as it relates to investigation and prosecution of offences alleged to have been committed under the Prevention of Corruption Act, 1988, shall stand transferred, along with its employees, assets and liabilities to Lokpal for all purposes.

(4) That part of Delhi Special Police Establishment, which has been transferred under sub-section (3), shall form part of Investigation Wing of Lokpal.

(5) The Central Government shall cease to have any control over the transferred part and its personnel.

(6) The salaries, allowances and other terms and conditions of services of the personnel transferred under sub-section (3) shall be the same as to which they were entitled to immediately before the commencement of this Act.

(7) All cases which were being dealt by that part of Delhi Special Police Establishment, which has been transferred under sub-section (3), shall stand transferred to Lokpal.

(8) After completion of investigation in any case, the investigation wing shall present the case to an appropriate bench of Lokpal, which shall decide whether to grant permission for prosecution or not.

26. Complaints against officers or employees of Lokpal.

(1) Complaints against employees or officers of Lokpal shall be dealt with separately and as per provisions of this section.

(2) Such complaint could relate to an allegation of an offence punishable under Prevention of Corruption Act or a misconduct or a dishonest enquiry or investigation.

(3) As soon as such a complaint is received, the same shall be displayed on the website of Lokpal, along with the contents of the complaint.

(4) Investigations into each such complaint shall be completed within a month of its receipt.

(5) In addition to examining the allegations against the said official, the allegations shall especially be examined against sections 107, 166, 167, 177, 182, 191, 192, 196, 199, 200, 201, 202, 204, 217, 218, 219, 463, 464, 468, 469, 470, 471, 474 of Indian Penal Code.

(6) If, during the course of investigations, the Lokpal feels that the charges are likely to be sustained, the Lokpal shall divest such officer of all his responsibilities and powers and shall place him under suspension.

(7) If after completion of enquiry or investigations, Lokpal decides to prosecute that person under Prevention of Corruption Act, 1988 or holds him guilty of any misconduct or of conducting dishonest enquiry or investigations, then that person shall not work with Lokpal anymore. Lokpal shall either dismiss that person from the job, if that person is in the employment of Lokpal, or shall repatriate him, if he is on deputation.

Provided that no order under this clause shall be passed without giving reasonable opportunity of being heard to the accused person.

Provided further that order under this clause shall be passed within 15 days of completion of investigations.

(8) There shall be a separate wing in Lokpal to deal with complaints against officers or staff of Lokpal.

(9) Lokpal shall take all steps to ensure that all enquiries and investigations on complaints against its own staff and officials are conducted in most transparent and honest manner.

27. Protection.

(1) No suit, prosecution, or other legal proceedings shall lie against the Chairperson or members or against any officer, employee, agency or person referred to in Section 14(4) in respect of anything which is in good faith done while acting or purporting to act in the discharge of his official duties under this Act.

(2) No proceedings of the Lokpal shall be held to be bad for want of form and except on the ground of jurisdiction, no proceedings or decision of the Lokpal shall be liable to be challenged, reviewed, quashed or called in question in any court of ordinary Civil Jurisdiction.

MISCELLANEOUS

28. Public Servants to submit property statements.

(1) Every public servant, other than those mentioned in Section 2(11)(a) to (c), shall within three months after the commencement of this Act and thereafter before the 30th June of every year submit to the head of that public authority, in the form prescribed by Lokpal, a statement of his assets and liabilities and those of the members of his family. Public servants mentioned in sections 2(11)(a) to (c) shall submit their returns in a format prescribed by the Lokpal to the Lokpal with the aforesaid time lines.

(2) The Head of each public authority shall ensure that all such statements are put on the website by 31st August of that year.

(3) If no such statement is received by the Head of that public authority from any such public servant within the time specified in sub-section (1), the Head of that public authority shall direct the concerned public servant to do so immediately. If within next one month, the public servant concerned does not submit such statement, the Head shall stop the salary and allowances of that public servant till he submits such statement.

Explanation: In this section "family of a public servant" means the spouse and such children and parents of the public servant as are dependent on him.

(4) The Lokpal may initiate prosecution against such public servant under Section 176 IPC.

(5) If any public servant furnishes any statement, which is subsequently found to be incorrect, then Lokpal, in addition to taking action against the

said public servant under other sections of this Act, may also impose a penalty upto a maximum of 50% of the value of the additional property subsequently detected. Lokpal shall also intimate such information to the Income Tax Department for appropriate action.

29. Power to delegate and assign functions.

(1) Lokpal shall be competent to delegate its powers and assign functions to the officials working in Lokpal.

(2) All functions carried out and powers exercised by such officials shall be deemed to have been so done by the Lokpal.

Provided that the following functions shall be performed by the benches and cannot be delegated: (i) Granting permission to initiate prosecution in any case. (ii) Order for dismissal of any government servant under CCS Conduct Rules. (iii) Passing orders under section 10 on complaints against officials and staff of Lokpal. (iv) Pass orders in cases of complaints, other than grievances, against officers of the level of Joint Secretary and above.

30. Time limits.

(1) Preliminary enquiry under sub-section (1) of section 9 of this Act should be completed within a month of receipt of complaint.

Provided that the enquiry officer shall be liable for an explanation if the enquiry is not completed within this time limit.

(2) Investigation into any allegation shall be completed within six months, and in any case, not more than one year, from the date of receipt of complaint.

(3) Trial in any case filed by Lokpal should be completed within one year. Adjournments should

be granted in rarest circumstances.

31. Penalty for false complaint.

(1) Notwithstanding anything contained in this Act, if someone makes any false or frivolous complaint under this Act, Lokpal may impose such fines on that complainant as it deems fit.

Provided that no fine can be imposed without giving a reasonable opportunity of being heard.

(2) Such fines shall be recoverable as dues under Land Revenue Act.

(3) A complaint or allegation once made under this Act shall not be allowed to be withdrawn.

31A. Preventive measures.

(1) Lokpal shall, at regular intervals, either study itself or cause to be studied the functioning of all public authorities falling within its jurisdiction and in consultation with respective public authority, issue such directions as it deems fit to prevent incidence of corruption in future.

(2) Lokpal shall also be responsible for creating awareness about this Act and involving general public in curbing corruption and maladministration.

32. Power to make Rules.

(1) The Government may, by notification in the Official Gazette, make rules for the purpose of carrying into effect the provisions of this Act.

Provided that such rules shall be made only in consultation and with the approval of Lokpal.

(2) In particular, and without prejudice to the generality of the foregoing provisions, such rules may provide for-

(i) the allowance and pensions payable to and other conditions of service of the Chairperson and members of Lokpal;

(ii) the powers of a Civil Court which may be exercised by the Lokpal under clause (h) of sub-section (2) of section 11;

(iii) the salary, allowances, recruitment and other conditions of service of the staff and employees of the Lokpal;

(iv) any other matter for which rules have to be made are necessary under this Act.

(3) Any rule made under this Act may be made with retrospective effect and when such a rule is made the reasons for making the rule shall be specified in a Statement laid before both Houses of the Parliament.

33. Removal of difficulties. Notwithstanding anything contained in this Act, the President, in consultation with Lokpal or on request of Lokpal may, by order, make such provision -

(i) for bringing the provisions of this Act into effective operation;

(ii) for continuing the enquiries and investigations pending before the Central Vigilance Commission by the Lokpal.

34. Power to make regulations. Lokpal shall have power to make its own regulations for the smooth functioning of the institution and to effectively implement various provisions of this Act.

35. This Act shall override the provisions of all other laws.

2

Campaign and Movement for the Jan Lokpal Bill

Introduction

The Jan Lokpal Bill, also referred to as the Citizens' Ombudsman Bill, is a proposed anti-corruption law in India. It was proposed by anti-corruption social activists as a more effective improvement to the original Lokpal bill, which is currently being proposed by the Government of India. The prefix *Jan* (translation: citizens) was added to signify the fact that these improvements include input provided by "Ordinary citizens" through an activist-driven, non-governmental public consultation.

The Jan Lokpal Bill aims to effectively deter corruption, redress grievances of citizens, and protect whistle-blowers. If made into law, the bill would create an independent ombudsman body similar to the Election Commission of India called the *Lokpal*. It would be empowered to register and investigate complaints of corruption against politicians and bureaucrats without prior government approval. First introduced in 1968, the bill has failed to become law for over four decades.

In 2011, Gandhian rights activist Anna Hazare started a Satyagraha movement by commencing a fast unto death in New Delhi to demand the passing of the bill. The movement attracted attention in the media, and thousands of supporters. Following Hazare's four day hunger strike, Indian Prime Minister Manmohan Singh stated that the bill would be re-introduced in the 2011 monsoon session of the Parliament.

Accordingly, a committee of five Cabinet Ministers and five social activists attempted to draft a compromise bill merging the two versions but failed. The Indian government went on to propose its own version in the parliament, which the activists reject on the grounds of not being sufficiently effective.

Background

The Lokpal bill was first introduced by Shanti Bhushan in 1968 and passed in the 4th Lok Sabha in 1969. But it did not get through in the Rajya Sabha, the upper house of the Parliament of India. Subsequent versions were re-introduced in 1971, 1977, 1985, 1989, 1996, 1998, 2001, 2005 and in 2008, but none of them passed.

Renewed calls for the bill arose over resentment of the major differences between the draft 2010 Lokpal Bill prepared by the government and that prepared by the members of the associated activists movement – N. Santosh Hegde, a former justice of the Supreme Court of India; Lokayukta of Karnataka; Shanti Bhushan; Arvind Kejriwal; Prashant Bhushan, a senior lawyer in the Supreme Court; and members of the India Against Corruption movement.

The bill's supporters consider existing laws too weak, full of contradictions and insufficiently empowered to combat corruption. On the other hand, critics of the Jan Lokpal Bill argue that the bill attempts to supercede existing constitutional bodies and attempts to create a super-institution with sweeping powers, which can be dangerous for the future of democracy.

Key Features of Proposed Bill

Some important features of the proposed bill are:

1. To establish a central government anti-corruption institution called *Lokpal*, supported by *Lokayukta* at the state level.
2. As in the case of the Supreme Court and Cabinet Secretariat, the *Lokpal* will be supervised by the Cabinet Secretary and the Election Commission. As a result, it will be completely independent of the government and free from ministerial influence in its investigations.
3. Members will be appointed by judges, Indian Administrative Service officers with a clean record, private citizens and constitutional authorities through a transparent and participatory process.
4. A selection committee will invite shortlisted candidates for interviews, video recordings of which will thereafter be made public.
5. Every month on its website, the *Lokayukta* will publish a list of cases dealt with, brief details of each, their outcome and any action taken or proposed. It will also publish lists of all cases received by the *Lokayukta* during the previous month, cases dealt with and those which are pending.
6. Investigations of each case must be completed in one year. Any resulting trials should be concluded in the following year, giving a total maximum process time of two years.
7. Losses caused to the government by a corrupt individual will be recovered at the time of conviction.
8. Government office work required by a citizen that is not completed within a prescribed time period will result in *Lokpal* imposing financial penalties on those

9. Complaints against any officer of *Lokpal* will be investigated and completed within a month and, if found to be substantive, will result in the officer being dismissed within two months.
10. The existing anti-corruption agencies (CVC, departmental vigilance and the anti-corruption branch of the CBI) will be merged into *Lokpal* which will have complete power and authority to independently investigate and prosecute any officer, judge or politician.
11. Whistleblowers who alert the agency to potential corruption cases will also be provided with protection by it.

Difference Between Government and Activist Drafts Highlights

Difference between Draft Lokpal Bill 2010 and Jan Lokpal Bill	
Draft Lokpal Bill (2010)	**Jan Lokpal Bill (Citizen's Ombudsman Bill)**
Lokpal will have no power to initiate *suo motu* action or receive complaints of corruption from the general public. It can only probe complaints forwarded by the Speaker of the Lok Sabha or the Chairman of the *Rajya Sabha.*	*Lokpal* will have powers to initiate *suo motu* action or receive complaints of corruption from the general public.
Lokpal will only be an Advisory Body with a role limited to forwarding reports to a "Competent Authority.	*Lokpal* will have the power to initiate prosecution of anyone found guilty.
Lokpal will have no police powers and no ability to register an FIR or proceed with criminal investigations.	*Lokpal* will have police powers as well as the ability to register FIR's.
The CBI and Lokpal will be unconnected.	Lokpal and the anti corruption wing of the CBI will be one independent body.
Pinishment for corruption will be minimum of 6 months and a maximum of upto 7 years.	Punishments will be a minimum of 10 years and a maximum of upto life imprisonment.

Campaign for the Jan Lokpal Bill

The first version of the Lokpal Bill drafted by the Government of India in 2010 was considered ineffective by anti-corruption activists from the civil society. These activists, under the banner of India Against Corruption, came together to draft a citizen's version of the Lokpal Bill later called the Jan Lokpal. Public awareness drives and protest marches were carried out to campaign for the bill. However, public support for the Jan Lokpal Bill draft started gathering steam after Anna Hazare, a noted Gandhian announced that he would hold an indefinite fast from April 5, 2011 for the passing of the Lokpal/Jan Lokpal bill.

Characteristics of Jan Lokpal Bill

- Non-violence
- Satyagraha
- Hunger strikes
- Civil resistance
- Civil disobedience
- Demonstrations
- Sit-ins
- Fast-unto-death
- Jail Bharo Andolan
- Online activism
- Candlelight vigil

To dissuade Hazare from going on an indefinite hunger strike, the Prime Minister's Office directed the ministries of personnel and law to examine how the views of society activists can be included in the Lokpal Bill. On April 5, the National Advisory Council rejected the Lokpal bill drafted by the government. Union Human Resource Development Minister Kapil Sibal then met social activists Swami Agnivesh and Arvind Kejriwal on 7 April to find ways to bridge differences

Detailed

The following table details differences between the Government and activist backed versions

Issue	The Jan Lokpal Bill	Government's Lokpal Bill
Prime Minister	Can be investigated with permission of seven member Lokpal bench.	PM can be investigated by Lokpal after s/he vacates office.
Judiciary	Can be investigated, though high level members may be investigated only with permission of a seven member Lokpal bench.	Judiciary is exempt and will be covered by a separate "judicial accountability bill".
MPs	Can be investigated with permission of seven member Lokpal bench.	Can be investigated, but their conduct within Parliament, such as voting, cannot be investigated.
Lower bureaucracy	All public servants would be included.	Only Group A officers will be covered.
Central Bureau of Investigation (CBI)	The CBI will be merged into the Lokapal.	The CBI will remain a separate agency.
Removal of Lokpal members and Chair	Any person can bring a complaint to the Supreme Court, who can then recommend removal of any member to the President.	Any "aggrieved party" can raise a complaint to the President, who will refer the matter to the CJI.
Removal of Lokpal staff and officers	Complaints against Lokpal staff will be handled by independent boards set-up in each state, composed of retired bureaucrats, judges, and civil society members.	Lokpal will conduct inquiries into its own behavior.

Lokayukta	Lokayukta and other local/state anti-corruption agency would remain in place.	All state anti-corruption agencies would be closed and responsiblities taken over by centralized Lokpal.
Whistleblower Protection	Whistleblowers are protected law.	No protection granted to whistleblowers.
Punishment for corruption	Lokpal can either directly impose penalties, or refer the matter to the courts. Penalties can include removal from office, imprisonment, and recovery of assets from those who benefited from the corruption.	Lokpal can only refer matters to the courts, not take any direct punitive actions. Penalties remain equivalent to those in currrent law.
Investigatory Powers	Lokpal can obtain wiretaps, issue rogatory letters, and recruit investigating officers. Cannot issue contempt orders.	Lokpal can issue contempt orders, and has the ability to punish those in contempt. No authority to obtain wiretaps, issue rogatory letters, or recruit investigating officers.
False, frivolous and vexatious complaints	Lokpal can issue fines for frivolous complaints (including frivolous complaints against Lokpal itself), with a maximum penalty of 1 lakh.	Court system will handle matters of frivolous complaints. Courts can issue fines of Rs. 25,000 to 2 lakh.
NGOs	NGOs not within the scope due to their role in exposing corruption.	NGOs are within the scope and can be investigated.
Scope	All corruption can be ivestigated.	Only high-level corruption can be investigated.

over the bill. However, no consensus could be reached on April 7 owing to several differences of opinion between the social activists and the Government.

On April 7, Anna Hazare called for a *Jail Bharo Andolan* from April 13 to protest against Government's rejection of their demands. Anna Hazare also claimed that his group has received six crore (60 million) text messages of support and that he had further backing from a large number of Internet activists. The outpouring of support was largely free of political overtones; political parties were specifically discouraged from participating in the movement. The fast ended on April 9, after 98 hours, when the Government accepted most demands due to public pressure. Anna Hazare set an August 15 deadline for the passing of the bill in the Parliament, failing which he would start a hunger strike from August 16. The fast also led to the Government of India agreeing to setting up a Joint Drafting Committee, which would complete its work by June 30.

However, the Joint Drafting Committee failed to reach a conclusion and the five members of the Government on the panel came up with their own version of the bill, which is considered by Anna as weak and will facilitate the corrupt to go free apart from several other differences. To protest against this, Anna Hazare announced an "indefinite fast" (not to be confused with "Fast unto Death"). Anna and his team asked for permission from Delhi Police for their fast and agitation at Jantar-Mantar or J P Park. Delhi Police gave its permission with certain conditions. These condition were considered by team Anna as restrictive and against the fundamental constitutional rights and they decided to defy the conditions. Delhi Police imposed sec 144 CrPC.

On Aug 16, Anna Hazare was taken into preventive custody by Delhi Police. Senior officers of Delhi Police reached Anna Hazare's flat early in the morning and informed him that he could not leave his home. However, Hazare turned down the request following which he was detained. Anna in his recorded address to the nation before his arrest asked his supporters not to stop the agitation and urged the protesters to remain peaceful. Other members of "India against Corruption", Arvind Kejriwal, Kiran Bedi and Manish Sisodia were also taken into preventive custody. Kiran Bedi described the situation as resembling a kind of Emergency (referring to the Emergency imposed in 1975).

The arrest resulted in huge public outcry and under pressure the government released him in the evening of Aug 16. However, Anna Hazare refused to come out of Jail, starting his indefinite fast from Jail itself. Manish Sisodia explained his situation as, "Anna said that he left home to go to JP Park to conduct his fast and that is exactly where he would go from here (Tihar Jail). He has refused to be released till he is given a written, unconditional permission". Unwilling to use forces owing to the sensitive nature of the case, the jail authorities had no option but to let Anna spend the night inside Tihar. Later on 17th Aug, Delhi Police permitted Anna Hazare and team to use the Ramlila Grounds for the proposed fast and agitation withdrawing most of the contentious provisions they had imposed earlier.

Notable Supporters and Opposition

In addition to the activists responsible for creating and organizing support for the bill, a wide variety of other notable individuals have also stated that they support this bill. Spiritual leaders Sri Sri Ravi Shankar and Yog Guru Ramdev expressed support. Notable politicians who indicated support for the bill include Ajit Singh and Manpreet Singh Badal as well as the principal opposition party, Bharatiya Janta Party. In addition, numerous Bollywood actors, directors, and musicians publicly approved of the bill.

Notable opposition to the citizens' version of the Bill was expressed by HRD minister Kapil Sibal and other Congress leaders; Chief Minister of West Bengal Mamta Banerjee; Punjab

Chief Minister and Akali Dal leader Prakash Singh Badal; Shiv Sena leader Bal Thackeray, and former Chief Justice of the Supreme Court Jagdish Sharan Verma. Although BJP showed their support earlier, there were reports that BJP shared Congress's concern "over letting the civil society gain the upper hand over Parliament in lawmaking".

Drafting Committee

The drafting committee was officially formed on 8 April 2011. It consisted of the following ten members, including five from the government and five drawn from the civil society.

Member	Qualifications and status
Pranab Mukherjee	Finance Minister, *Co-Chairman*
Shanti Bhushan	Former Minister of Law and Justice, *Co-Chairman*
P. Chidambaram	Minister of Home Affairs
Veerappa Moily	Minister of Corporate Affairs
Kapil Sibal	Minister for Communications and Information Technology
Salman Khursid	Minister of Law
Anna Hazare	Social Activist
Prashant Bhushan	Lawyer
N. Santosh Hegde	Former Lokayukta (Karnataka) and
Arvind Kejriwal	RTI Activist.

The Government's handling of the formation of the draft committee, involving the civil society in preparation of the draft Lokpal bill, was criticized by various political parties including BJP, BJD, TDP, AIADMK, CPI-M, RJD, JD(U) and Samajwadi Party.

The committee failed to agree on the terms of a compromise bill and the government introduced its own version of the bill in the parliament in August 2011.

Criticisms of the Bill

Naïve Approach: The bill has been criticized as being naïve in its approach to combating corruption. According to Pratap Bhanu Mehta, President of the Center for Policy Research Delhi writes that the bill *"is premised on an institutional imagination that is at best naïve; at worst subversive of representative democracy"*. The very concept of a Lokpal concept has received criticism from HRD minister Kapil Sibal in that it will lack accountability, be oppresive and undemocratic.

Extra Constitutional: The pro-bill activist Arvind Kejriwal rejects the claim of Lokpal being extra-constitutional with the explanation that the body will only investigate corruption offences and submit a charge sheet which would then tried and prosecuted through trial courts and higher courts. And that other bodies with equivalent powers in other matters exist. And also that the proposed bill also lists clear provisions for the Supreme Court to abolish the Lokpal.

Despite these clarifications, critics feel that the exact judicial powers of Lokpal are rather unclear in comparison with its investigative powers. The bill requires *"...members of Lokpal and the officers in investigation wing of Lokpal shall be deemed to be police officers"*. Although some supporters have denied any judicial powers of Lokpal the government and some critics have recognized Lokpal to have quasi-judicial powers.

The bill also states that *"Lokpal shall have, and exercise the same jurisdiction powers and authority in respect of contempt of itself as a High court has and may exercise, and, for this purpose, the provisions of the Contempt of Courts Act, 1971 (Central Act 70 of 1971)shall have the effect subject to the modification that the references therein to the High Court shall be construed as including a reference to the Lokpal."* Review of proceedings and decisions by Lokpal is prevented in the bill by the statement *"...no proceedings or decision of the Lokpal shall be liable to be challenged, reviewed, quashed or called in question in any court of ordinary Civil Jurisdiction."*. As a result, how the trials will be conducted is unclear in the bill, although the bill outlines requiring judges for special courts, presumably to conduct trial that should be completed within one year. The critics hence express concern that, without judicial review, Lokpal could potentially become an extra-constitutional body with investigative and judicial powers whose decisions cannot be reviewed in regular courts.

Scope

The matter of whether the Indian Prime Minister and higher judiciary should or should not be prosecutable by the Lokpal remains as one of the major issues of dispute. Anna's own nominee for co-chairing the joint panel Justice Verma, the former Chief Justice of the Supreme Court, has expressed his constitutional objections for including the Prime Minister and higher judiciary under Lokpal. According to him, "*this would foul with the basic structure of the constitution*".

Criticism from Aruna Roy & NCPRI

Magsaysay Award winner Aruna Roy has said "*Vesting jurisdiction over the length and breadth of the government machinery in one institution will concentrate too much power in the institution, while the volume of work will make it difficult to carry out its tasks*". She and her colleagues at the National Campaign for People's Right to Information (NCPRI) have proposed an alternative mechanism consisting of five institutions.

Controversies

In April 2011, the involvement of the bill co-chairman Shanti Bhushan was questioned after a CDROM emerged with audio clippings of a telephone conversation allegedly between him, Mulayam Singh Yadav and Amar Singh about influencing a judge. All involved reacted to the allegation saying that the CD was fabricated and demanded a formal investigation to verify its authenticity.

On August 16, 2011 Hazare was arrested at his residence by Delhi Police just as he was leaving for the JP Park to commence his indefinite hunger strike. He was arrested on the grounds that his protest would cause law and order problems in the city. The police also simultaneously arrested Arwind Kejriwal and other supporters. Large crowds gathered in protest of this action forcing the police to detain thousands. Many in the city also participated in a candle light protest at India Gate in response.

3

Civil Society Members of Jan Lokpal Bill

Introduction

The Jan Lokpal Bill (Citizen's Ombudsman Bill) is a draft anti-corruption bill drawn up by prominent civil society activists seeking the appointment of a Jan Lokpal, an independent body that would investigate corruption cases, complete the investigation within a year and envisages trial in the case getting over in the next one year.

It is drafted by Justice Santosh Hegde (former Supreme Court Judge and former Lokayukta of Karnataka), Prashant Bhushan (Supreme Court Lawyer) and Arvind Kejriwal (RTI activist), the draft Bill envisages a system where a corrupt person found guilty would go to jail within two years of the complaint being made and his ill-gotten wealth being confiscated. It also seeks power to the Jan Lokpal to prosecute politicians and bureaucrats without government permission.

Retired IPS officer Kiran Bedi and other known people like Swami Agnivesh, Sri Sri Ravi Shankar, Anna Hazare and Mallika Sarabhai are also part of the movement, called India

Against Corruption. Its website describes the movement as "an expression of collective anger of people of India against corruption. We have all come together to force/request/persuade/pressurize the Government to enact the Jan Lokpal Bill. We feel that if this Bill were enacted it would create an effective deterrence against corruption."

Anna Hazare, anti-corruption crusader, went on a fast-unto-death in April, demanding that this Bill, drafted by the civil society, be adopted. Four days into his fast, the government agreed to set up a joint committee with an equal number of members from the government and civil society side to draft the Lokpal Bill together. The two sides met several times but could not agree on fundamental elements like including the PM under the purview of the Lokpal. Eventually, both sides drafted their own version of the Bill.

The government has introduced its version in Parliament in this session. Team Anna is up in arms and calls the government version the "Joke Pal Bill." Anna Hazare declared that he would begin another fast in Delhi on August 16. Hours before he was to begin his hunger strike, the Delhi Police detained and later arrested him. There are widespread protests all over the country against his arrest.

ANNA HAZARE

Anna Hazare was born on 15 January 1940 in Bhingar village in Ahmednagar district of Maharashtra state in western India to Baburao Hazare and Laxmi Bai, an unskilled labourer family.

He was raised by his childless aunt in Mumbai but could not continue beyond VII standard and had to quit midway due to problems.

Anna Hazare was not driven to such a pass by circumstances. He wanted to live no more because he was frustrated with life and wanted an answer to the purpose of human existence.

1963 -

Anna had enrolled with the Army on April 14, 1963.

1. He had completed his training at Aurangabad in Maharashtra.
2. He had joined the service as a recruit.
3. He was attested as a soldier on November 16, 1963.
4. He was holding the rank of sepoy at the time of leaving the service.

Anna Hazare started his career as a driver in the Indian Army.

During his 15-year tenure as a soldier, he was posted to several states like Sikkim, Bhutan, Jammu-Kashmir, Assam, Mizoram, Leh and Ladakh and braved challenging weathers.

When Anna was in Army five medals were notified to Anna –

1. Sainya Seva Medal,
2. Nine Years Long Service Medal,
3. Sangram Medal,
4. 25th Independent Anniversary Medal
5. Paschimi Star

Anna was greatly influenced by Swami Vivekananda's teachings.

In the year 1965, Pakistan attacked India and at that time, Hazare was posted at the Khemkaran border. On November 12, 1965, Pakistan launched air attacks on Indian base and all of Hazare's comrades became martyrs.

In 1978, he took voluntary retirement from the 9th Maratha Battalion.

After serving 15 Years in Army, Anna took the voluntary retirement and returned to his native place in Ralegan Siddhi, in the Parner tehsil of Ahmednagar district.

Ralegan Siddhi falls in the drought-prone area with a mere 400 to 500 mm of annual rainfall.

There were no weirs to retain rainwater.

During the month of April and May, water tankers were the only means of drinking water.

Almost 80 per cent of the villagers were dependent on other villages for food grains. Residents used to walk for more than four to six kilometers in search of work

Hazare came across the work of one Vilasrao Salunke, a resident of Saswad near Pune who had started a novel project of water management through watershed development in a joint venture with the Gram Panchyat. Hazare visited the project and decided to implement it in Ralegan Siddhi.

He steered the villagers to begin working towards water conservation.

At the outset, they completed 48 Nala Bunding work, contour trenches, staggered trenches, gully plugs, meadows development and of forestation of 500 hectares of land. Thereafter, they constructed five RCC weirs and 16 Gabion Weirs.

This resulted in increase in the ground water level.

Hazare's Ralegan Siddhi became the first role model of an ideal village – from the worst village to an ideal village.

Anna rightly thought that Development is marred by corruption and started a new venture in 1991 called Bhrashtachar Virodhi Jan Aandolan (BVJA) or public movement against corruption.

It was found that some 42 forest officers had duped the state government for crores of rupees through corruption in confederacy.

Hazare submitted the evidences to the government but the latter was reluctant to take action against all these officers as one of the ministers of the ruling party was involved in the scam.

A distressed Hazare returned the Padmashree Award to the President of India and also returned the Vriksha Mitra Award given by then prime minister of India Rajiv Gandhi.

He further went on an indefinite hunger strike in Alandi on the same issue.

Finally, the government woke up and took action against the criminal and corrupt officers as well as six of the ministers were forced to resign and more than 400 officers from different government offices were sent back to home.

In 1995 Shiv Sena-BJP government came to power in the state. Hazare raised the issue of alleged massive land purchase by Gholap's wife Shashikala in Nashik between April to September 1996.

He forwarded the available documentary evidences in support of his allegations to then Maharashtra Governor P. C. Alexander.

On 4 November 1997, Gholap filed a defamation suit against Hazare for accusing him of corruption.

On 9 September 1998, Anna Hazare was imprisoned in the Yerawada Jail after being sentenced to simple imprisonment for three months by the Mumbai Metropolitan Court, all political parties, every one from Maharashtra except the BJP and the Shiv Sena came in support of him.

Later due to public protest, outcry the Government of Maharashtra ordered his release from the jail.

The state government has opened cooperative societies, credit societies & urban banks everywhere in states.

However, the directors of such societies do the corruption and failed to pay back the basic amount to the members of the societies.

Thus poor people get cheated when Anna saw this he again began his agitation against this.

Hazare agitated for over eight months.

The result was that more than Rs 125 crore was recovered from defaulters and the members of such societies heaved a sigh of relief.

Recovery of around Rs. 400 crores is in the pipeline.

After this Anna started to fight for the Right to information act.

Government ignored Anna.

In 1997 Anna agitated in Azad Maidan in Mumbai to create mass public awareness about RTI amongst the youth.

Anna started to travel across state.

Government promised Anna they will pass RTI act but in reality they never did it.

For this Anna agitated ten times for this law.

When Anna saw that Government is not willing to pass this law Anna went on an indefinite hunger strike at Azad Maidan in the last week of July 2003.

After 12 days of Hunger strike in Azad Maidan the President of India signed the draft of the Right to Information Act and ordered the state government to implement it with effect from 2002. The same draft was considered as the base document for the making of the National Right to Information Act-2005.

In 2003 Anna Hazare raised corruption charges against 4 ministers of the Congress-NCP government and Government ignored him.

Then Anna started his fast unto death agitation on 9 August 2003.

He ended his fast on 17 August 2003 after then chief minister Sushil Kumar Shinde formed a one man commission, headed by the retired justice P. B. Sawant to probe his charges.

The P. B. Sawant commission report was submitted on 23 February 2005, indicted Suresh Jain, Nawab Malik and Padmasinh Patil. Suresh Jain and Nawab Malik resigned from the cabinet in March 2005

Jan Lokpal Bill –

Agitation and hunger strike at the age of 73 and great victory against powerful and rich government.

India against corruption movement:

N. Santosh Hegde, a former justice of the Supreme Court of India and Lokayukta of Karnataka, Prashant Bhushan, a senior lawyer in the Supreme Court along with the members of the India against Corruption movement drafted an alternate bill, named as the Jan Lokpal Bill (People's Ombudsman Bill) with more stringent provisions and wider power to the Lokpal (Ombudsman) .

On April 5, 2011 Again Anna started second freedom struggle in India.

Anna wrote to everyone regarding Jan Lok Pal bill but no one listened him.

After that on 5th April 2011, Started fast unto death to wake up the government for India.

Anna started war against corruption in India.

Hazare has started a fast unto death from 5 April 2011 at Jantar Mantar in Delhi, to press for the demand to form a joint committee of the representatives of the Government and the civil society to draft a new bill with stronger penal actions and more independence to the Lokpal and Lokayuktas (Ombudsmen in the states).

In beginning Government of India ignored him, many people said many things, but as First day was over Anna got the support from every corner of India and no one has expected such a support Anna will get for this bill.

Over night table were turned and after 4 days of discussion with government of India servants.

Finally Prime Minister of India Manmohan Singh realized that demand of Anna is right and government accepted all the demands of Anna.

Thus Jantar Mantar saved from becoming another Tahir Square.

Anna Hazare won the following awards –

1. Indira Priyadarshini Vrikshamitra award by the

Government of India on November 19, 1986 from the hands of Prime Minister of India Rajiv Gandhi.

2. 1989 - Krishi Bhushana award by the Government of Maharashtra.
3. 1990 - Padmashri award, by the Government of India.
4. 1992 - Padmabhushan award, by the Government of India.
5. 2008 - On April 15 2008, Anna Hazare received the World Bank's 2008 Jit Gill Memorial Award for Outstanding Public Service.
6. Care International of the USA, Transparency International, Seoul (South Korea).
7. He received awards worth Rs 25 lakh and donated the entire amount for the Swami Vivekananda Kritadnyata Nidhi (social gratitude fund). Out of the two lakh rupees received from the above amount, mass marriages are carried of at least 25-30 poor couples every year.

Anna Hazare has given his life for the benefit of India.

He got the home in his village but he has not entered in that house from last 35 years.

Anna Hazare and Properties –

Anna Hazare has declared he has got Rs. 68, 688 in bank balance and cash and three pieces of land.

Hazare's lands were either donated to him or family owned.

In his statement, Hazare said two land pieces measuring 0.07 Hectares and two hectares are in his native village in Ralegan Siddhi in Maharashtra while 0.46 hectare of land is in Pimpianer.

One of the pieces of land in Ralegan Siddhi was donated by Army to him which he has donated for village use.

The Pimpianer land was donated to him by a villager. Hazare has further donated this land for village use.

Today, Anna Hazare is the face of India's fight against corruption. He has taken that fight to the corridors of power and challenged the government at the highest level. People, the common man and well-known personalities alike, are supporting him in the hundreds swelling to the thousands.

The Gandhian is soldiering on. From one battle to another in his war against corruption. He fought from the front to have Right to Information (RTI) implemented. He is now fighting for the implementation of the Jan Lokpal Bill, the anti-corruption bill drafted by his team of crusaders.

This year, more than 30 years after Anna Hazare started his crusade, as the 74-year-old plans a second hunger strike in Delhi against large-scale corruption at the national level. Nothing really has changed except the scale of his battle.

ARVIND KEJRIWAL

Arvind Kumar Kejriwal born on 16 June 1968 is an Indian social activist fighting for greater transparency in Government. He was awarded Ramon Magsaysay Award for Emergent Leadership in 2006, for activating India's Right to Information movement at grassroots and social activities to empower the poorest citizens to fight corruption by holding the government answerable to the people. Kejriwal is also a Saathi (fellow) of the Association for India's Development.

Early life

Arvind Kejriwal was born in Hissar, Haryana in 1968. His father was an engineer and he spent most of his childhood living in small northern Indian towns like Sonepat, Mathura and Hissar. Kejriwal graduated from IIT Kharagpur as a Mechanical engineer in 1989.

Career

Kejriwal joined Tata Steel after his graduation from IIT Kharagpur. After quitting his job with Tata Steel, he took time off to work with the Missionaries of Charity and the Ramakrishna Mission in the northeast.

Kejriwal joined the Indian Revenue Service (IRS) in 1995 and worked as an Additional Commissioner of Income Tax in Delhi. In January 2000, he took a sabbatical from work and founded Parivartan a Delhi based citizens' movement which works on ensuring a just, transparent and accountable governance. Thereafter, in February 2006, he resigned from the job, to work full-time at 'Parivartan'.

Right to Information

He along with Aruna Roy and others, campaigned for the Right to Information Act, which soon became a silent social movement, Delhi Right to Information Act was passed in 2001 and eventually at national level Indian Parliament passed the Right to Information Act (RTI) in 2005. Thereafter, in July 2006, he spearheaded an awareness campaign for RTI across India. To motivate others. Arvind has now instituted an RTI Award through his organisation. Through individual and community cases, Arvind has taken on many deeply entrenched public bureaucracies in India, including the Income Tax department, the Municipal Corporation of Delhi, the Public Distribution System (PDS), the Delhi Electricity Board, and others.

Jan Lokpal Bill

As a member of India Against Corruption, Kejriwal is an active participant in the movement for the enactment of Jan Lokpal Bill. He is considered a key figure along with social activist Anna Hazare. On August 16 2011, Hazare was arrested four hours before the planned indefinite hunger strike. Rajan Bhagat, spokesman for Delhi Police, said police arrested Hazare under a legal provision that bans public gatherings and protests at the park in Delhi where he was planning to begin his hunger strike. Kejriwal was also arrested along with other key members of the India against Corruption movement.

Personal Life

Kejriwal is married to Sunita, who is an IRS officer and his batchmate from training academy in Mussoorie. They live just outside Delhi with their two children.

Awards

- 2004: Ashoka Fellow, Civic Engagement.
- 2005: 'Satyendra Dubey Memorial Award', IIT Kanpur for his campaign for bringing transparency in Government.
- 2006: Ramon Magsaysay Award for Eminent Leadership.
- 2006: CNN-IBN, 'Indian of the Year' in Public Service.
- 2009: Distinguished Alumnus Award, IIT Kharagpur for Eminent Leadership.
- 2010: Policy Change Agent of the Year, Economic Times Corporate Excellence Award along with Aruna Roy.

Books

The Right to Information: Vyawharik Margdarshika - Co-Author - Vishnu Rajgadia, Published by Rajkamal Prakashan, New Delhi in the year 2008.

SHANTI BHUSHAN

Shanti Bhushan (born 11 November 1925) is a former Law Minister of India at Ministry of Law and Justice (1977–1979) in the Morarji Desai Ministry and also a senior advocate. He along with his son Prashant Bhushan was featured at 74th position in a list of the most powerful Indians published by The Indian Express in 2009.

Political Career

Bhushan was an active member of Congress (O) party and later the Janata Party. He was a member of the Rajya Sabha from 14 July 1977 to 2 April 1980 and the Union Law minister in the Morarji Desai ministry from 1977 to 1979. He joined the Bhartiya Janata Party in 1980. In 1986, he resigned from BJP after the party acted against his advice over an election petition.

As the then Law Minister, he introduced the Lokpal bill in 1977. However, it did not pass because of the collapse of the government. He is presently co-chairman of the joint committee constituted in April 2011 for the Jan Lokpal Bill.

Prominent Cases and Clients

- Bhushan represented Raj Narain in a case against Indira Gandhi, the then Prime Minister of India. Justice Jagmohan Lal Sinha judged Indira Gandhi guilty and declared her election to the Lok Sabha void. The decision resulted in widespread political protests and ultimately resulted in the declaration of a state of emergency in India.
- In 1994, he appeared for two of the defendants accused of participating in the 1993 Mumbai bomb blasts case.
- In 2002, he appeared as a counsel for Arundhati Roy in a contempt case against her in the Supreme Court of India.
- Bhushan represented Shaukat Hussain Guru in 2008 for an appeal against his 10 year conviction for his role in the 2001 Indian Parliament attack.
- Bhushan appeared as senior counsel for Transparency International in the Provident Fund scandal case of Ghaziabad, which allegedly involved several judges of the Indian judiciary. The bench abandoned the hearing after deeming his remarks as contemptuous and termed his behavior as that of a street urchin.
- Shanti Bhushan was the counsel for the former Prime Minister of India H. D. Deve Gowda in a petition related to allocation of land for Bangalore - Mysore Infrastructure Corridor.

- He has represented Rajendra Singh Lodha regarding the assets of Birla Corporation.
- He represented V.S.Achuthanandan in the Supreme Court in the Idamalayar Dam corruption case against UDF leader R.Balakrishna Pillai and others. The bench awarded rigorous imprisonment for one year with fine of Rs. 10,000/- each to the accused persons.

Activism

Shanti Bhushan, along with his son Prashant Bhushan has been involved in accountability of the Indian Judiciary by setting up Campaign for Judicial Accountability and Judicial Reform (CJAR). The campaign has been responsible for action against the judicial misconduct of Yogesh Kumar Sabharwal and for the declaration of assets by the judges.

The campaign had also protested against the actions and appointments of Justice S. Ashok Kumar, Madan Mohan Punchhi, Soumitra Sen and Ashwini Kumar Mata.

The father-son duo are currently facing contempt of court at Supreme Court of India for their statement about corruption in higher judiciary specifically, former chief justices of Supreme Court.

During a hearing on the running case for contempt of court in November 2010, Shanti Bhushan went on to say:

> *"The question of apology does not arise. I am prepared to go to jail."*

Works

Courting Destiny: A Memoir (2008)

PRASHANT BHUSHAN

Prashant Bhushan born in 1956 is an Indian lawyer and social activist. He is the son of eminent lawyer Shanti Bhushan. He lives in Noida.

He is an activist who helps people through the judiciary system. In his career of 15 years he has worked on around 500 PILs (Public Interest Litigation). He is a strong supporter of a Clean Judiciary.

He is a member of the committee constituted in April 2011 for the Jan Lokpal bill.

Education

He studied in IIT Madras, which he quit after a semester in Mechanical Engineering. He studied economics and then philosophy (of science) at Princeton.

Works

He is the author of two books:

- 1. The Case that Shook India.
- 2. Bofors, The Selling of a Nation.

N. SANTOSH HEGDE

Nitte Santosh Hegde born on June 16, 1940 is a former justice of the Supreme Court Of India, former Solicitor General of India and was Lokayukta (Ombudsman) for Karnataka State of India from 2006-2011.

Early life

Santosh Hegde was born in Udupi district in Karnataka to former speaker of Loksabha, Justice K. S. Hegde and his wife Meenakshi Hegde. He is one of six children born to the couple who belong to the Bunt. He was born on 16 June 1940 in Nitte, Udupi district, Karnataka. He had his early education at St. Aloysius College, Mangalore and Madras Christian College in Madras. He completed his intermediate exam from St. Joseph's College, Bangalore and B. Sc degree from Central College of Bangalore. Hegde graduated with a law degree from Government Law College (now known as University Law College), Bangalore in 1965.

Career

After completing apprenticeship training, he enrolled as an advocate in January 1966 and was designated as senior advocate in May 1984. Hegde was appointed as the Advocate General for the state of Karnataka in February 1984 and held that position till August 1988. He worked as additional Solicitor General of the Union of India from December 1989 to November 1990 and was re-appointed as the Solicitor General of India on 25-04-1998. Nitte Santosh Hegde was appointed as a judge of Supreme Court of India on 08-01-1999. He retired as judge of Supreme Court of India in June 2005. He was conferred honorary doctorate of law degree by Mangalore University in 2005. For a brief period, he worked as Chairperson of Telecom Dispute Settlement Appellate Tribunal, New Delhi. Hegde was of the view that Telecom Regulatory Authority of India (TRAI) was not the authority for dispute resolution between customers and telecommunication service providers. He was appointed as Lokayukta of Karnataka state on 3 August 2006 for a term of five years.

Major Anti-corruption Cases and Investigations as Lok Ayukta of Karnataka

The Lok Ayukta had exposed major irregularities in mines in Bellary, including those owned by Obulapuram Mining Company and by G. Karunakara Reddy, G. Janardhana Reddy and G. Somashekara Reddy who are ministers in the Government of Karnataka. He has expressed concern about illegal mining taking place in state of Karnataka which have deep repercussion for ecology and to exchequer of state. A report constituted by the Lok Ayukta uncovered major violations and systemic corruption in iron-ore mining in Bellary. There were violations in the allowed geography, encroachment of forest land, massive underpayment of state mining royalties relative to the market price of iron ore and systematic starvation of government mining entities. The damage to public interest was so serious that he recommended banning all exports of iron ore and limiting iron ore production for captive production of iron and steel.

Controversies

- He was alleged to have pressured Chief Minister of Karnataka to remove then Bruhat Bangalore Mahanagara Palike (BBMP) commissioner S. Subramanya. Subramanya was heading the BBMP which was held responsible for bad maintenance of Bangalore, including drowning accidents during monsoon.
- Some people have questioned his political motives in timing his resignation a day before a BJP state government convention, though he has not been aligned with any particular political party over the course of his career.

Resignation from Post of Lok Ayukta

Hegde resigned from the Lokayukta position on 23 June 2010 after an honest officer (Deputy Conservator of Forests R Gokul) was suspended by order of minister J. Krishna Palemar and he felt powerless to help. He expressed inability to be effective in his anti-corruption mandate owing to a non-cooperative Government of Karnataka. After the resignation, he stated:

> A cabinet minister wanted an officer to be suspended for having exposed attempts to export illegal iron ore from Belekeri port that was seized by our team in a raid on March 20. When the officer sought my help, I could not do anything. Besides this, all officers against whom I conducted raids and suspended, have been reinstated.

Amid media speculation that the ports minister Palemar had recommended Gokul's suspension on behalf of some politicians with business interests, Palemar defended his recommendation to suspend Gokul since he failed to attend a meeting, for it raised suspicions that he may be involved in the scam himself. In fact, in a press meeting, Hegde indicated that:

The whole idea was if Gokul is suspended even for a day, a new investigating officer can be appointed and a scam of this stature which runs to thousands of crores can be shut. I couldn't do anything for Gokul who had done the investigation going out of his way. I was very disturbed and couldn't sleep for two days. I told my wife and decided to resign on Wednesday.

The matter, which is being called the Belekeri port scam, relates to 3.5 million tons of illegal iron ore, belonging to the powerful mining lobby headed by G. Janardhana Reddy, that was ready to be exported from Belekeri port. After Gokul seized the ore and the high court refused to permit it's export without appropriate papers, a large part of it was surreptitiously exported from the port. Hegde's resignation sought to underline the helplessness of the advisory post of the Lokayukta in such situations.

After persistent protests and public pressure, Karnataka Chief Minister Yeddyurappa admitted to an illegal iron-ore export racket at Belekeri Port involving 35 lakh metric tonnes of iron ore.

Justice Hegde withdrew his resignation and agreed to continue in the post of Lok Ayukta after persuasion from National leadership of the BJP. The party risked a major loss of face in the BJP ruled Karnataka State government by allowing an upright person in public service to leave office, though All India Congress Committee general secretary B K Hariprasad said that "Hegde's actions prove that he is a BJP man".

He retired as Lokayukta of Karnataka on 2 August 2011. His successor is Justice Shivraj Patil.

KIRAN BEDI

Kiran Bedi born on 9 June 1949 is an Indian social activist and a retired 1972 batch Indian Police Service officer. She held the post of Director General at the Bureau of Police Research and Development before she voluntary retired from the IPS in December 2007.

She has also founded two NGOs in India: Navjyoti for welfare and preventive policing in 1987 and the India Vision Foundation for prison reformation, drug abuse prevention and child welfare in 1994. She is one of the winners of the 2011 Bharatiya Manavata Vikas Puraskar.

Early Life and Education

Kiran Bedi was born in Amritsar, Punjab, India. She is the second of the four daughters of Prakash Peshawaria and Prem Peshawaria.

She attended the Sacred Heart Convent School, Amritsar, where she joined the [National Cadet Corps (India)]. She took up tennis, a passion she inherited from her father, a tennis player. She won the Junior National Lawn Tennis Championship in 1966, the Asian Lawn Tennis Championship in 1972, and the All-India Interstate Women's Lawn Tennis Championship in 1976. In addition, she also won the All-Asian Tennis Championship, and won the Asian Ladies Title at the age of 22.

She earned her Bachelor of Arts in English (Hons.) from the Government College for Women, Amritsar in 1968. She then earned a Master's degree in Political Science from Punjab University, Chandigarh, graduating at the top of her class in 1970. She later obtained Bachelor of Laws in 1988 from University of Delhi. In 1993, she obtained a Ph.D. in Social Sciences from the Department of Social Sciences, Indian Institute of Technology, New Delhi, where the topic of her thesis was 'Drug Abuse and Domestic Violence'.

Career

She began her career as a Lecturer in Political Science (1970-72) at Khalsa College for Women, Amritsar. In July 1972, she joined the Indian Police Service, becoming the first woman to do so. Bedi joined the police service "because of her urge to be outstanding".

She served in a number of tough assignments ranging from New Delhi traffic postings, Deputy Inspector General of Police in insurgency prone Mizoram, Advisor to the Lieutenant Governor of Chandigarh, Director General of Narcotics Control Bureau, to a United Nations delegation, where she became the Civilian Police Advisor in United Nations Peacekeeping Operations. For her work in the UN, she was awarded a UN medal. She is popularly referred to as *Crane Bedi* for towing the Prime Minister Indira Gandhi's car for a parking violation, during the PM's tour of United States at the time.

Kiran Bedi influenced several decisions of the Indian Police Service, particularly in the areas of narcotics control, traffic management, and VIP security. During her stint as the Inspector General of Prisons, in Tihar Jail (Delhi) (1993-1995), she instituted a number of reforms in the management of the prison, and initiated a number of measures such as detoxification programs, Art of Living Foundation Prison Courses, yoga, vipassana meditation, Murat redressing of complaints by prisoners and literacy programs. For this she won the 1994 Ramon Magsaysay Award, and the 'Jawaharlal Nehru Fellowship', to write about her work at Tihar Jail.

She was last appointed as Director General of India's Bureau of Police Research and Development.

In May 2005, she was awarded an honorary degree of Doctor of Law in recognition of her "humanitarian approach to prison reforms and policing".

On 27 November 2007, she had expressed her wish to voluntarily retire from the police force to undertake new challenges in life. On 25 December 2007, the Government of India agreed to relieve Bedi of her duties as Director General of the Bureau of Police Research and Development.

"Yes Madam, Sir", an award-winning, critically acclaimed film of Kiran Bedi's life, directed by Australian director, Megan Doneman, premiered as an official selection at the Toronto International Film Festival. It has yet to be released.

Honours, Awards and International Recognition

Year of Award or Honor	Name of Award or Honor	Awarding Organization
2010	STAR Parivar Award	STAR Plus
2005	Mother Teresa Memorial National Award	Indian Development Foundation (IDF)
2004	United Nations Medal	United Nations
2002	Woman of the Year Award	Blue Drop Group Management, Cultural and Artistic Association, Italy.
1999	Pride of India Award	American Federation of Muslims of Indian Origin (AFMI)
1997	Fourth Joseph Beuys Award	Germany
1995	Lion of the Year	
1995	Father Machismo Humanitarian Award	Don Bosco Shrine Office, Bombay-India
1995	Mahila Shiromani Award	
1994	Magsaysay Award	Ramon Magsaysay Award Foundation
1991	Asia Region Award for Drug Prevention and Control	International Organisation of Good Templars (IOGT), Norway
1981	Women of the Year Award	National Solidarity Weekly, India
1979	President's Gallantry Award	President of India

Lokpal Movement

Kiran Bedi is one of the prominent members of the Anna Hazare team which is on a nationwide protest against corruption and is urging the government to enact the Lokpal Bill and has conducted numerous protests and demonstrations throughout the country in the last year.

On Aug 16th 2011, Kiran Bedi Courted Arrest as part of the agitation called for by Anti Graft activist Anna Hazare of which Kiran Bedi is one of the frontline members. However, she was later released in the evening.

Manish Sisodia

Manish Sisodia born on 5 January 1972 is an Indian social activist, recognized for being a key member in the 2011 Indian anti-corruption movement. Formerly a news producer at Zee News, Manish is an active RTI activist. He is the co-founder of Kabir and with Arvind Kejriwal of Public Cause Research Foundation, NGOs aimed at creating awareness about Indian laws like the RTI.

A look at the salient features of Jan Lokpal Bill:

1. An institution called LOKPAL at the centre and LOKAYUKTA in each state will be set up
2. Like Supreme Court and Election Commission, they will be completely independent of the governments. No minister or bureaucrat will be able to influence their investigations.
3. Cases against corrupt people will not linger on for years anymore: Investigations in any case will have to be completed in one year. Trial should be completed in next one year so that the corrupt politician, officer or judge is sent to jail within two years.
4. The loss that a corrupt person caused to the government will be recovered at the time of conviction.

5. How will it help a common citizen: If any work of any citizen is not done in prescribed time in any government office, Lokpal will impose financial penalty on guilty officers, which will be given as compensation to the complainant.
6. So, you could approach Lokpal if your ration card or passport or voter card is not being made or if police is not registering your case or any other work is not being done in prescribed time. Lokpal will have to get it done in a month's time. You could also report any case of corruption to Lokpal like ration being siphoned off, poor quality roads been constructed or panchayat funds being siphoned off. Lokpal will have to complete its investigations in a year, trial will be over in next one year and the guilty will go to jail within two years.
7. But won't the government appoint corrupt and weak people as Lokpal members? That won't be possible because its members will be selected by judges, citizens and constitutional authorities and not by politicians, through a completely transparent and participatory process.
8. What if some officer in Lokpal becomes corrupt? The entire functioning of Lokpal/ Lokayukta will be completely transparent. Any complaint against any officer of Lokpal shall be investigated and the officer dismissed within two months.
9. What will happen to existing anti-corruption agencies? CVC, departmental vigilance and anti-corruption branch of CBI will be merged into Lokpal. Lokpal will have complete powers and machinery to independently investigate and prosecute any officer, judge or politician.
10. It will be the duty of the Lokpal to provide protection to those who are being victimized for raising their voice against corruption.

Movement and Agitation against Lokpal Bill

In 2011, Hazare initiated a Satyagraha movement for passing a stronger anti-corruption Lokpal (Ombudsman) bill in the Indian Parliament as conceived in the Jan Lokpal Bill (People's Ombudsman Bill). The Jan Lokpal Bill was drafted earlier by N. Santosh Hegde, former justice of the Supreme Court of India and Lokayukta of Karnataka, Prashant Bhushan, a senior lawyer in the Supreme Court and Arvind Kejriwal, a social activist along with members of the India Against Corruption movement. This draft bill incorporated more stringent provisions and wider power to the *Lokpal* (Ombudsman) than the draft Lokpal bill prepared by the government in 2010. These include placing "the Prime Minister within the ambit of the proposed lokpal's powers".

Hunger Strike in Delhi

Hazare began his fast unto death on 5 April 2011 at Jantar Mantar in Delhi to press for the demand to form a joint committee of the representatives of the Government and the civil society to draft a stronger anti-corruption bill with stronger penal actions and more independence to the *Lokpal* and *Lokayuktas* (Ombudsmen in the states), after his demand was rejected by the Prime Minister of India Manmohan Singh. He stated, "I will fast until Jan Lokpal Bill is passed".

The movement attracted attention in the media, and thousands of supporters. Almost 150 people reportedly joined Hazare in his fast. Social activists, including Medha Patkar, Arvind Kejriwal, former IPS officer Kiran Bedi, and Jayaprakash Narayan lent their support to Hazare's hunger strike and anti-corruption campaign. People have shown support in Internet social media such as Twitter and Facebook. Online Signature Campaigns like avaaz got 6.5 lakh signatures in just 36 hours. In addition to spiritual leaders Sri Sri Ravi Shankar, Swami Ramdev, Swami Agnivesh and former Indian cricketer Kapil Dev, many celebrities showed their public support through Twitter. Hazare decided that he would not allow any politician to sit with him in this movement. Politicians like Uma Bharti and Om Prakash Chautala were shooed away by the protesters when they came to visit the site where the protest was taking place. On 6 April 2011, Sharad Pawar resigned from the *group of ministers* formed for reviewing the draft Lokpal bill 2010.

The movement gathered significant support from India's youth, visible through the local support and on social networking sites like Facebook and Twitter. Protests spread to Bangalore, Mumbai, Chennai, Ahmedabad, Guwahati, Shillong, Aizawl and a number of other cities in India.

End of Hunger Strike after Meeting Demands

On 8 April 2011, the Government of India accepted all demands of the movement. On 9 April 2011, it issued a notification in the Gazette of India on formation of a joint committee. It accepted the formula that there be a politician Chairman and an activist, non-politician Co-Chairman. According to the notification, Pranab Mukherjee will be the Chairman of the draft committee while Shanti Bhushan will be the co-chairman. "The Joint Drafting Committee shall consist of five nominee ministers of the Government of India and five nominees of the civil society. The five nominee Ministers of the Government of India are Pranab Mukherjee, Union Minister of Finance, P. Chidambaram, Union Minister of Home Affairs, M. Veerappa Moily, Union Minister of Law and Justice, Kapil Sibal, Union Minister of Human Resource and Development and Minister of Communication and Information Technology and Salman Khursheed, Union Minister of Water Resources and Minister of Minority Affairs. The five nominees of the civil society are Anna Hazare, N. Santosh Hegde, Shanti Bhushan Senior Advocate, Prashant Bhushan, Advocate and Arvind Kejriwal.

On the morning of 9 April 2011, Hazare ended his 98-hour hunger strike by first offering lemon juice to some of his supporters who were fasting with him. Hazare then broke his fast by consuming some lemon juice. He addressed the people and set a deadline of 15 August 2011 to pass the Lokpal Bill in the Indian Parliament.

"Real fight begins now. We have a lot of struggle ahead of us in drafting the new legislation. We have shown the world in just five days that we are united for the cause of the nation. The youth power in this movement is a sign of hope."

Anna Hazare said that if the bill does not pass he will call for a mass nation-wide agitation. He called his movement as "second struggle for independence" and he will continue the fight.

Differences with the Government on Draft Bill

During the meeting of the joint drafting committee on 30 May 2011, the Union government members opposed the inclusion of the prime minister, higher judiciary and the acts of the MPs under the purview of the Lokpal in the draft bill. On 31 May 2011, Pranab Mukherjee, chairman of the joint drafting committee sent a letter to the chief ministers of all states and the leaders of the political parties seeking their opinion on six contentious issues in the proposed Lokpal Bill, including whether to bring the prime minister and judges of Supreme Court and High Courts under the purview of the proposed law. But the civil society members of the drafting committee considered that keeping the prime minister and judges of Supreme Court and High Courts out of the purview of the Lokpal would be a violation of the United Nations Convention against Corruption.

Anna Hazare and other civil society members decided to boycott the meeting of the joint Lokpal Bill drafting committee scheduled on 6 June 2011 in protest against the forcible eviction of Swami Ramdev and his followers by the Delhi Police from

Ramlila Maidan on 5 June 2011, while they were on hunger strike against the issues of black money and corruption and doubting seriousness of the government in taking measures to eradicate corruption.

On 6 June 2011, the members of the civil society of the joint Lokpal bill drafting committee in New Delhi sent a letter to Pranab Mukherjee, the chairman of the committee, explaining reasons for their absence at the meeting and also asked government to make its stand public on the contentious issues related to the proposed draft legislation. They also decided that the future meetings will be attended only if they were telecast live. On 8 June 2011 at Rajghat, describing his movement as the second freedom struggle, Anna criticised the Government for trying to discredit the joint Lokpal Bill drafting committee and threatened to go on indefinite fast again from 16 August 2011 if the Lokpal Bill is not passed by then. He also criticised the Government for putting hurdles in the drafting of a strong Lokpal Bill and its attempts to malign the civil society members of the joint Lokpal panel.

Indefinite Fast

On 28 July 2011, the union cabinet approved a draft of the Lokpal Bill, which keeps the Prime Minister, judiciary and lower bureaucracy out of the ambit of the proposed corruption ombudsman Lokpal. Hazare rejected the government version by describing it as "cruel joke" and wrote a letter to Prime Minister Manmohan Singh, and told him his decision to go on an indefinite fast from 16 August 2011 at Jantar Mantar if the government introduced its own version of the bill in Parliament without taking suggestions from civil society members.

Why are you (government) sending the wrong draft? We have faith in Parliament. But first send the right draft, our agitation is against government, not Parliament. The government has overlooked many points. How will it fight corruption by excluding government employees, CBI and Prime minister from the Lokpal's purview? We were told that both the drafts would be sent to the Cabinet. But only the government's draft was sent. This is a deceitful government. They are lying. How will they run the country? Now I have no trust in this government. If it is really serious about fighting corruption, why is it not bringing government employees and CBI under Lokpal?- *Anna Hazare*

Within twenty four hours of cabinet's endorsement of a weak Lokpal Bill, over ten thousand peoples from across the country sent faxes directly to the government demanding a bill with stronger provisions. The Mumbai Taxi Men's Union, comprises over 30,000 taxi drivers have extended their full support to Hazare's fast by keeping all taxis off the roads on 16 August 2011. Lawyers of Allahabad High Court described Lokpal Bill proposed by the government as against the interest of the country and pledged their support to Hazare by hunger strike at Allahabad on 16 August 2011. On 30 July 2011 Vishwa Hindu Parishad supported Hazare's indefinite fast by saying movement for an effective anti-corruption ombudsman needs the backing of people.

On 1 August, Public interest litigation was filed in the Supreme Court of India by Hemant Patil, a Maharashtra-based social worker and businessman, to restrain Hazare from going on his proposed indefinite fast. The petitioner demanded to prohibit the fast alleging that Hazare's demands are unconstitutional and amount to interference in legislative process.

Arrest and Aftermath

On 16 August 2011, Hazare was arrested four hours before the planned indefinite hunger strike. Rajan Bhagat, spokesman for Delhi Police, said police arrested Hazare under a legal provision that bans public gatherings and protests at the park in Delhi where he was planning to begin his hunger strike. Police took that action after Hazare refused to meet the conditions put forward by police for allowing the protest. The conditions included restricting the length of the fast to three days and the number of protesters at the site to 5,000. Later Anna was sent to Tihar jail under judicial custody for 7 days. After announcements by Prashant Bhushan (Hazare's lawyer), local television, and social media sites (including Facebook), a march of thousands in support of Hazare began from the India Gate to Jantar Mantar.

Along with Hazare, other key members of the India Against Corruption movement including Arvind Kejriwal, Shanti Bhushan, Kiran Bedi and Manish Sisodia were also detained from different locations. It was reported that about 1,300 supporters were detained in Delhi. Media also reported that the arrest sparked off protests with people courting arrests in different parts of the country. The opposition parties in the country came out against the arrest, likening the government action to the emergency imposed in the country in 1975. Both the houses of Parliament were adjourned over the issue.

Eventually, after being kept in judicial detention for 24 hours, he was released by police, but Hazare and his supporters refused to sign bail bond and he was sent to Tihar Jail. They demanded permission to observe a fast in support of the Janlokpal bill, without any conditions. Hazare continued his fast inside the jail.

After his arrest, Anna Hazare received massive support from people across the country. There were reports of "nearly 570 demonstrations and protests by Anna supporters across the country" against the government's imprisonment of Hazare and others. Due to the nationwide protests of millions, the Indian government agreed to release Hazare from jail and allow him to begin a public hunger strike of fifteen days. After talks with public authorities. Hazare decided to hold his protest at Ramlila Maidan, New Delhi. On 20 August 2011, Hazare "left the Tihar Jail for the Ramlila Grounds". Hazare promised reporters "he would fight to the 'last breath' until the government gets his team's Jan Lokpal Bill passed in this session of Parliament, which ends on 8 September."

Fast at Ramlila Maidan

On August 20, 2011 thousands came to the Ramlila Maidan to show their support for Hazare, while "his advisers made televison appearances to rally public support and defend themselves against criticism that their protest campaign and refusal to compromise is undermining India's parliamentary process." The National Campaign for People's Right to Information (NCPRI) condemned Hazare's deadline for passing the bill as undermining democracy, which operates by "holding wide-ranging consultations and discussions, allowing for dissent and evolving a consensus. He [Hazare] has the right to protest and dissent. But nobody can claim it as an absolute right and deny the right of dissent to others." The Congress party confirmed that Maharashtra Additional Chief Secretary (Home) Umesh Chandra Sarangi (who has a history of mediating between Hazare and government officials) was meeting with the social activist again "to find points of consensus and defuse the situation". On August 21, 2011 "tens of thousands" came to Ramlila Maidan to support Hazare as he sat on an elevated platform. It was reported that Hazare at that point had "lost more than seven pounds since beginning his fast", despite this he stated "'I will not withdraw my hunger strike until the Jan Lokpal bill is passed in the Parliament. I can die but I will not bend.'"

Electoral Reform Movement

In 2011, Anna Hazare demanded an amendment to the electoral law to incorporate the option of None of the above in the electronic voting machines during the Indian elections. The "None of the above (NOTA)" is a ballot option that allows an electorate to indicate disapproval of all of the candidates in an electoral system, in case of non-availability of any candidate of his choice, as his Right to Reject. Soon, the Chief Election Commissioner of India, Shahabuddin Yaqoob Quraishi supported Hazare's demand for the electoral reforms.

Protest Against Atrocities against Swami Ramdev and his Supporters

On 8 June 2011, Anna Hazare and thousands of his supporters observed fast from 10 am to 6 pm at Rajghat to protest against the midnight crackdown of 5 June 2011 by the Delhi Police on Swami Ramdev's fast at Ramlila Maidan, New Delhi. The fast was initially planned to be held at Jantar Mantar, but the venue was shifted after the denial of permission by the Delhi police. Anna Hazare held the Prime Minister of India responsible for the atrocities and termed the police action as a blot on humanity and an attempt to stifle democracy. According to one of the Anna's young supporters, the large presence of youths in the protest was due to their support to his use of nonviolence means of protest similar to Gandhi.

Controversies and Criticism

Views on Narendra Modi: In a press conference in April 2011, Anna Hazare praised Narendra Modi, the chief minister of Gujarat for his efforts on rural development along with Nitish Kumar, chief minister of Bihar, saying that the same should be emulated by the chief ministers of all states. Subsequently, Modi wrote an open letter to him, hailing him as a Gandhian and anti-corruption activist while Digvijay Singh, the General Secretary of the Congress party, criticised him for his comment. In May 2011, Hazare, during his visit to Gujarat, changed his view and criticised Modi for rampant corruption by Government officials in Gujarat. He urged Modi to appoint a Lokayukta in Gujarat. He also commented that the media had projected an incorrect image of Vibrant Gujarat, very different from the prevalent situation.

Accusations of Corruption

The government of the state of Maharashtra instituted a Commission of Inquiry under Justice PB Sawant in September 2003 to enquire into allegations of corruption against several people, including four ministers in the state as well as the "Hind Swaraj Trust" headed by Hazare. The Commission submitted its report on 22 February 2005 in which it indicted the Hind Swaraj Trust for corrupt practice of spending Rs. 2.20 lakhs of its funds on the birthday celebrations of Hazare. Two days ahead of Hazare's proposed indefinite fast on 16 August 2011, the ruling party of India, the Indian National Congress, launched an attack on him alleging that "the moral core of Hazare has been ripped apart" by the Justice P B Sawant Commission.

In response to this allegation, Hazare's lawyer Milind Pawar, claimed that the commission had remarked about "irregularities" in the accounts, but had not held him guilty of any "corrupt" practices. Pawar said that on 16 June 1998, a celebration was organised to facilitate Hazare on winning an award from a US based NGO and it coincided with his 61st birthday. The trust spent Rs 2.18 lakh for the function. Abhay Phirodia, a Pune-based industrialist, who took the initiative to organise this function donated an amount of Rs 2,48,950 to the trust by cheque soon after the function.

Hazare himself responded to the allegation by daring the government to file a First Information Report (FIR) against him to prove the charges.

Accusation of Being Anti-democratic and Anti-dalit

Dalit columnists like Chandrabhan Prasad have opined that the movement initiated by Anna Hazare against corruption and for lokpal bill is taking us to a situation of rejecting representative democracy and also alleged that this movement is an upper-caste uprising against India's political democracy. It is also alleged that the centralization of such huge powers in Lokpal which is a non-elected entity will lead the democratic setup to a very dangerous situation.

Dalit activist Kancha Ilaiah also commented in a similar fashion, that "The Anna movement is an anti-social justice, manuvadi movement. The Dalits, tribals, OBCs and minorities have nothing to do with it. We oppose it." Another activist Anoop Kheri claimed that "The language, symbols used by the movement clearly reflects its upper caste Hindu nature, a very rightwing Hindu patriotism is being used to get the entire country against corruption. And as a dalit, I have a problem with it."

There was also an allegation that an RTI activist was denied permission to protest by having a fast-unto-death at Ralegan Siddhi, by the grama sabha stating the reason that only Anna Hazare can hold such fasts in his village.

4

Principles of Jan Lokpal Bill and Powers of Lokpal

In addition to the Basic principles given earlier, we submit some more principles below:

Amendments to "Basic principles of Jan Lokpal Bill" submitted on 2nd May 2011:

1. Replace 6(b) in the document titled "Basic principles of Jan Lokpal Bill"

To receive complaints of misconduct against bureaucrats and recommend appropriate penalties under conduct rules. However, the recommendation shall be binding on the government.

After investigations into any case, Lokpal shall have powers to impose departmental penalties after giving an opportunity of being heard on government servants. The opportunity may be given by either a bench of Lokpal members or by a bench of Lokpal officers. Appeal against this order shall lie in High Court. Ordinarily, High Courts shall not stay the order. However, if it does, it will have to decide the case within two months, else the stay would be deemed to have been vacated after two months and no further stay on that order could be granted.

2. Delete 6(c), which reads as: For complaints against any politician for his/her conduct inside Parliament, Lokpal shall only investigate the matter on receipt of a reference from Chairperson of either House. After investigation, the Lokpal shall submit its report to Chairperson, who shall present it in the House for decision on the same.

Its deletion would mean that we want conduct of MPs within Parliament, if it is an offence under Prevention of Corruption Act, also to be covered.

Additions to "Basic principles of Jan Lokpal Bill" submitted on 2nd May 2011: Public grievances:

3. Important points on Vigilance Officers, citizens' charters and grievances:

a. Only those grievances which can be resolved in time bound manner will make it to citizen's charter.

b. Violation of citizen's charter would lead to compulsory imposition of departmental penalties on the officer concerned, the Head of the Department and any other officer who, through his act of omission or commission, did not redress the grievance in time. The penalty will be imposed by a bench of Lokpal members or a bench of some of its officers in open hearings.

c. Citizen's charter should be made within a year of enactment of this law by each department.

   If any department fails to do so, the Lokpal/Lokayukta will have powers to notify the same, which shall be binding on that department.

d. In this one year, the government will require all departments to make an assessment of the manpower or other resources required to implement citizen's charter. The government shall provide those resources before the implementation of citizen's charter.

e. The government would make appropriate amendments in their rules and laws to give powers to Heads of Departments to procure and provide such resources as may be required by his officers to properly implement citizen's charters.

f. When the grievance reaches Head of Department, he should be able to resolve it at his level. Suitable amendments would be made in various laws to enable Heads of Departments to be able to do that.

g. Annual review of the charter provisions in public hearings, where head of that department, the public and representatives of Lokpal/Lokayukta will be present. The charter will be finalized by the end of the public hearing.

h. Proceedings before Vigilance officer should be in open hearings.

i. A social audit of each VO shall take place every six months, in which he shall present himself before the public, present the data related to his functioning, respond to public queries and incorporate suggestions from public in his functioning. The public hearing shall be attended by a senior officer from Lokpal/ Lokayukta.

j. Vigilance Officers could have geographical jurisdiction. There could be one Vigilance Officer of Lokpal in each district (However this could change depending upon the concentration of central government offices in that area); however, there must be at least one VO for each block for Lokayukta.

k. No case can be closed by VO till the citizen's grievance is redressed or the case is rejected by Lokpal.

l. Every Head of a public authority shall be responsible for framing its own citizen's charter. Lokpal shall have powers to impose penalties against the head of a public authority if he fails to make citizen's charter in time.

4. In addition to the points mentioned in the citizen's

charter, in those cases where corruption is established, the Lokpal will have power to order grievances and wrong doings associated with that case redressed.

Financial independence of Lokpal:

5. Annual funds as required and demanded by Lokpal shall be provided. However, that amount shall not exceed 0.5% of total annual budget.

Checks and balances of Lokpal system:

6. Any complaint against a Vigilance officer shall be heard by an independent complaints authority to be set up in each state (in larger states more than one complaints authority could also be set up). The authority shall consist of five to ten members from diverse backgrounds to be selected through a transparent and participatory process. The authority will hear complaints in open hearings. If the authority so orders, the vigilance officer shall be removed from the job.

7. Not more than 5% cases should exceed one year limit of investigations and no case should exceed 18 months time limit. In rarest of rare cases, a case shall be allowed to be investigated beyond 18 months only with the approval of a bench of Lokpal members.

8. CAG would annually audit Lokpal/Lokayukta.

9. Annual appraisal by appropriate Parliamentary Committee.

Powers of Lokpal:

10. If during investigations, Lokpal/Lokayukta feels that a government servant may affect the investigations in any manner or could cause further loss to the government through his corruption, Lokpal/Lokayukta may order his transfer.

11. Evidence shall be examined on the basis of the principle of preponderance of probabilities for imposition of departmental penalties. However, in imposing those penalties, a bench of Lokpal members or officers will give reasonable opportunity of being heard to the concerned officer and pass necessary orders. This procedure will replace all existing

procedures.

12. Detailed reasons shall be recorded by Investigating Officer before registering any case or before closing any case.

13. IO shall have powers under Prevention of Money Laundering Act and FEMA while investigating any case under PC Act.

14. Lokpal, and no other authority, shall be responsible for investigating cases mentioned in Paragraph 5 of Part B of the Schedule to Prevention of Money Laundering Act and for doing so, Lokpal shall have all the powers under that Act.

15. Lokpal shall be designated as Central Authority for the purposes of mutual legal assistance. (Declaration notification recently presented by India for ratifying the UN Convention against Corruption needs to be accordingly modified and Lokpal should be included as the designated central authority under article 46 (13) of the convention for affecting mutual legal assistance.)

16. Lokpal shall exercise the powers and responsibilities of the central government in respect of the letters of request under sections 166A and 166B of the code of criminal procedure, so far as they relate to offences under the Prevention of Corruption Act as well as the connected offences.

17. Protection against prejudicial treatment - Lokpal shall have powers to get a grievance solved if any person is harassed due to making a complaint to Lokpal or to get a grievance of a complainant resolved who has suffered because of corruption in that case.

Miscellaneous:

18. If charges are framed by the court in any case, then the accused shall not be eligible for fighting elections till acquitted. However, if convicted, then they shall not be eligible for fighting elections for lifetime.

19. If convicted, an elected representative will be deemed to have vacated his seat.

20. If any company or its officer or its Director are

convicted under this Act, that company and all companies promoted by any of that company's promoters shall be blacklisted and be ineligible for undertaking any government work or contract in future.

21. After an investigation, a case would be filed in a trial court for prosecution. For all other orders of Lokpal/ Lokayukta, the appeal would lie in High Court. Ordinarily, High Courts shall not stay the order. However, if it does, it will have to decide the case within two months, else the stay would be deemed to have been vacated after two months and no further stay in that case could be granted.

22. In addition to having powers and duty to provide protection to whistleblowers, Lokpal shall also do so for victims of corruption and witnesses in cases being investigated by Lokpal.

23. Section 4 (4) of Prevention of Corruption Act shall be amended as - "Notwithstanding anything contained in the Code of Criminal Procedure, 1973 a Special Judge shall hold the trial of an offence on day-to-day basis, and shall not grant adjournment for any purpose unless such adjournment is, in its opinion, necessary in the interests of justice and for reasons to be recorded in writing"

24. Relocation of section 19 (3) (c) of Prevention of Corruption Act as new Section 4 (5) as- "Notwithstanding anything contained in the Code of Criminal Procedure 1973, i) no court shall stay the special court proceedings under this Act, and ii) no court shall exercise the powers of revision in relation to any interlocutory order passed in any inquiry, trial appeal or other proceedings".

25. Lokpal will have a duty to lay down a sentencing policy.

26. The Chief Justices of a High Courts will constitute special benches in respective High Courts to hear cases only under this Act. Such number of benches shall be constituted so as to ensure that appeal in any case under this Act is decided as expeditiously as possible and not later than six months.

27. The judges of Special Courts and the appellate benches set up by High Courts to hear cases under this Act will deal only with cases under this Act and will not deal with any other cases.

Application of certain sections of CrPC:

28. The provisions of sections 105C to 105I of CrPC shall apply to offences under PC Act whether or not they are transnational in nature or not.

29. Section 389(3) of CrPC shall not apply to offences under Prevention of Corruption Act.

30. Power of state to file appeals under section 377 of CrPC shall be exercised by Lokpal.

31. Under section 372 of CrPC, power to file an appeal should be given to complainant also (under this section, complainant shall be deemed to be a victim)

BASIC PRINCIPLES OF JAN LOKPAL BILL

There should be an institution called Jan lokpal at the centre and Jan Lokayukta in each state.

The following points are being written for Jan Lokpal. However, exactly similar model would be applicable for states.

Independence of these institutions:

1. These institutions shall be financially, functionally and administratively independent of the government:

   a. *Financial Independence:* Their expenses shall be charged to the Consolidated Fund of India/state. They shall not need administrative or financial sanctions from any government agency for making expenditure. The quantum of expenses should be decided in an annual meeting between the Prime Minister and the Chairperson of Lokpal.

   b. *Control over their Employees:* They shall have the freedom to decide the number of employees required. They will have the power to select and recruit people either from outside or on deputation or on contract basis or through any arrangement as they deem fit.

2. The Chairperson and members shall not be eligible for appointment to any position in any organization, which is directly or indirectly funded by any government. It shall also not be eligible to contest any elections. The total tenure of any member or Chairperson or together as member and Chairperson shall not exceed five years.

Selection of members and Chairperson of Lokpal and Lokayukta:

3. The process should be completely transparent and participatory. There could be a very broad based selection committee, which may consist of constitutional authorities, including representatives from judiciary, bureaucracy and judiciary. This committee may be assisted by a search committee.

4. The new members should be selected at least three months before the retirement of any member.

Removal of members and Chairperson of Lokpal and Lokayukta:

5. If prima facie case is made out in a complaint made to the Supreme Court by a citizen against any member or Chairperson, Supreme Court shall institute a time bound enquiry and advise the President on the basis of such enquiry. A member or Chairperson of Lokpal may be removed by the President on the basis of such advice.

Jurisdiction:

6. Lokpal should have jurisdiction the following jurisdiction:

a. To receive complaints of corruption under Prevention of Corruption Act against Prime Minister, all ministers, all members of both houses of Parliament, all bureaucrats and judges of Supreme Court and High Court; to investigate these complaints and to file prosecution in appropriate trial courts for prosecution and award of punishment.

b. To receive complaints of misconduct against bureaucrats and recommend appropriate penalties under conduct rules. However, the recommendation shall be binding on the government.

c. For complaints against any politician for his/her conduct inside Parliament, Lokpal shall only investigate the matter on receipt of a reference from Chairperson of either House. After investigation, the Lokpal shall submit its report to Chairperson, who shall present it in the House for decision on the same.

7. Lokpal shall not need to seek permission from any other agency for initiating investigation, enquiry or prosecution. Appropriate amendments would need to be made in Prevention of Corruption Act and Delhi Police Establishment Act for this purpose.

Powers of Lokpal and Lokayuktas:

8. Lokpal and Lokayukta shall have powers of search and seizure as provided in .....

9. It shall have powers of a civil court to summon and seek production of documents under.....

10. It shall have powers of contempt and imposition of financial penalties to seek compliance of its orders.

11. It shall have powers to tap telephones under Indian telegraph Act.

12. It shall be deemed to be a police officer.

13. It shall have the powers to recommend, on an annual basis, the number of special courts required under section 4 of Prevention of Corruption Act, to ensure that the trial in any case is completed in less than a year. The recommendations shall be binding on the government.

14. It shall have the powers to issue letter rogatory, wherever required, in connection with investigations of cases under this Act.

15. Notify list of moveable and immoveable assets of accused, if during or at the time of conclusion of investigations,

Lokpal believes that prosecution is likely to be initiated. These assets cannot be transferred after such notification. Loss to exchequer quantified at the time of conviction, could be recovered from sale of these assets.

16. Recommend stay of any activity, if during investigations, Lokpal is satisfied that the allegations against such activity are likely to be sustained.

17. Recommend transfer of any official, if his continuance is likely to adversely affect investigations.

18. Powers to issue appropriate directions to prevent destruction of records during investigations, prevent further further acts of misconduct by a public servant or to prevent the public servant from secreting the assets allegedly acquired by him through corrupt means.

19. If the allegations are substantiated after any enquiry or investigations, recommend removal of any minister (barring Prime Minister).

20. Lokpal shall have powers to delegate any of its powers and functions barring those which are specifically to be performed by the benches of Lokpal.

Internal transparency and accountability of Lokpal:

21. Every complaint shall have to be compulsorily disposed by Lokpal. No complaint could be disposed without giving an opportunity of being hear to the complainant. If any case is closed, all records related thereto shall be made public.

22. There shall be complete transparency during investigations also. However, such records, which could impede the process of investigations, would not be disclosed. But after the completion of any investigation or enquiry, all records related to a case, shall be made public.

23. Lokpal shall publish, every month on its website, the status of cases, received, disposed, closed, reasons for closure and list of cases pending.

24. Any complaint against a staff of Lokpal shall be enquired into within a month of its receipt and if found correct, the staff shall be summarily dismissed from the job. If any criminal case is made out, the same shall be pursued.

Punishments and recovery of loss to the government:

25. At the time of conviction, the court shall make an assessment of the loss caused by the accused, which shall be recovered from them.

26. The minimum punishment shall be raised to one year of rigorous imprisonment and maximum should be raised to life imprisonment.

27. Punishment shall be higher if the status or rank of accused is higher.

28. If the beneficiary is a business entity, five times the loss caused to the government shall be recovered. The recovery may be done from the assets of that entity or the personal assets of its directors.

29. If any person obtains any benefit from the government in violation of any rules or laws, that person along with concerned public servants shall be deemed to have indulged in corrupt means.

Whistleblower protection:

30. Lokpal shall be responsible for providing protection against professional or physical threat or victimization to whistleblowers, whether within or outside the government.

Public grievances with vigilance angle:

31. Every department shall prepare a citizens charter mentioning which work will be done by which officer in how much time. Each department shall also designate the Head of the Department or a sufficiently senior officer as Public Grievance Officer (PGO). Violation of citizen's charter will be dealt by PGO, who will be required to get the work done in 30 days. If PGO also fails, the grievance will go to Vigilance Officer (who will be part of the Lokpal) and the grievance

will be deemed to have a vigilance officer. The vigilance officer shall get the work done in next 30 days, impose penalties on the guilty officers which will be paid as compensation to the citizen and proceed with enquiries of misconduct against guilty officers.

CBI, CVC and departmental vigilance:

32. The anti-corruption wing of CBI, the CVC and departmental vigilance wings of all departments will be merged in Lokpal.

Declaration of annual property statements:

33. Each bureaucrat, politician and judge would be required to submit his/her statement of moveable and immoveable assets on an annual basis, which will be put on a website.

34. If any asset is subsequently found to be owned by a public servant, which was not declared, it would be deemed to have been obtained through corrupt means.

35. If any asset is subsequently found to be in possession of any public servant, it shall be deemed to be owned by him/her unless he proves otherwise.

36. After each elections, the Lokpal shall verify the assets declared by each candidate with his declared sources of income in his tax returns. Those undeclared shall be investigated against.

CAG to forward cases of corruption:

37. CAG, after its report has been laid in the Parliament, shall forward such cases to Lokpal, where it feels that an offence under Prevention of Corruption Act is made out. Such cases shall be investigated by Lokpal.

Power to make Rules:

38. No rules shall be made without the approval of Lokpal. Lokpal shall have power to make rules and regulations with respect to its own functioning.

Transparency and applicability of Right to Information Act to Lokpal:

39. All records of Lokpal shall be open barring the following:

a. Such portions of any records which if released during any ongoing investigations, could impede the process of investigations. However, after completion of investigations, they would be disclosed.
b. Such records which could affect national security or
c. Such records which would disclose the identity of a whistleblower and could compromise his/her security.

Fines for frivolous complaints:

40. If anyone makes a complaint which lacks any evidence or basis and is held by Lokpal to be meant only to harass someone, the complainant shall be fined. However, merely closure of a case due to lack of evidence shall not be held against a complainant.

NOTES ON THE THIRD MEETING OF THE JOINT DRAFTING COMMITTEE - MAY 7, 2011

(*Please note that the five Civil Society members of the Drafting Committee have prepared these notes*)

The third meeting of Joint Drafting Committee (JDC) held on Sat. May 7, 2011 was a cordial meeting.

At the second meeting held on 2nd May, a document containing basic principles of Jan Lokpal Bill were presented to the government. The first few of these were discussed in Saturday's meeting.

Mr. Chidambaram took the lead to express the government's views. Some of the points discussed at the meeting in the table on next page.

Presently, if there is an allegation of corruption against a High Court or Supreme Court Judge, permission has to be taken from the Chief Justice of India to register an FIR.

Proposal	Discussion/ Decision
Independence of Lokpal:	
The institution of Lokpal should be financially, functionally and administratively independent of the government	Agreed in principal
Their expenses shall be charged to the Consolidated Fund of India/state. They shall not need administrative or financial sanctions from any government agency for making expenditure.	Agreed
The quantum of expenses should be decided in an annual meeting between the Prime Minister and the Chairperson of Lokpal.	The government representatives pointed out that in a coalition government it is possible that the PM and the Finance Minister might be from different parties. So what might be acceptable to the PM may not be acceptable to the Finance Minister. The JC agreed to study the CAG, the Supreme Court and other models for financial autonomy.
Control over their employees: Lokpal should have the freedom to decide the number of employees required. They will have the power to select and recruit people either from outside or on deputation or on contract basis or through any arrangement as they deem fit.	Agreed in principle. Government agreed to give SC kind of autonomy to Lokpal. It was agreed to study all available models to find best model suited for Lokpal.
The Chairperson and members shall not be eligible for appointment to any position in any organization, which is directly or indirectly funded by any government.	Agreed

It shall also not be eligible to contest any elections.	Would it be possible through statute or a constitutional amendment would be required - this needs to be examined
The total tenure of any member or Chairperson or together as member and Chairperson shall not exceed five years.	Agreed
Selection of members and Chairperson of Lokpal:	
The process should be completely transparent and participatory. Selection committee should consist of Prime Minister, Leader of opposition, two youngest judges of SC, two youngest Chief Justices of High Courts, CAG and CEC	Agreed but may suggest some more inclusions for selection committee after further examination
Since selection committee members would be very busy, they should be assisted by a search committee.	Agreed
Search committee should consist of retired constitutional authorities like CAG and CEC (CJI may not agree to work under a selection committee). However, those who have had substantive allegations of corruption, or have had affiliations to any political party or are still in any government employment after retirement should not be eligible for being members of search committee.	Government wants complete freedom to be given to selection committee to appoint anyone to search committee. However, civil society reps felt that this could compromise the independence of search committee. This matter would be discussed further.
Selection committee should restrict its choices to the names suggested by search committee	This needs further discussions

Removal of Lokpal:	
If prima facie case is made out in a complaint made to the Supreme Court by a citizen against any member or Chairperson, Supreme Court shall institute a time bound enquiry and advise the President on the basis of such enquiry. A member or Chairperson of Lokpal may be removed by the President on the basis of such advice.	Government suggested that Supreme Court should be allowed to dismiss complaints in liminae. Government further suggested that Article 317 which provides for removal of members of UPSC may be borrowed here with the exception that in the case of UPSC members, SC can act only on the basis of reference from the government whereas in the case of Lokpal, SC should be required to act on citizen's complaints also. What should be grounds of removal? All these issues would need further examination.
Jurisdiction of Lokpal:	
Lokpal should have jurisdiction the following jurisdiction: 1. To receive complaints of corruption under Prevention of Corruption Act against Prime Minister, all ministers, all members of both houses of Parliament, all bureaucrats and judges of Supreme Court and High Court; to investigate these complaints and to file prosecution in appropriate trial courts for prosecution and award of punishment. 2. To receive complaints of misconduct against bureaucrats and recommend appropriate penalties under conduct rules. However, the recommendation shall be binding on the government.	Broadly government agreed to jurisdiction over elected representatives including ministers. However, the issue of Prime Minister needs further discussion. On the issue of bureaucracy, it needs to be discussed whether Lokpal should have jurisdiction over all categories of employees. On the issue of judiciary, government said that there were strong opinions on this issue, especially two former Chief Justices had opposed jurisdiction over judiciary. There was a lot of discussion on this issue. Please see below for the same. All these issues need further examination.

3. For complaints against any politician for his/her conduct inside Parliament, Lokpal shall only investigate the matter on receipt of a reference from Chairperson of either House. After investigation, the Lokpal shall submit its report to Chairperson, who shall present it in the House for decision on the same.	
Lokpal shall not need to seek permission from any other agency for initiating investigation, enquiry or prosecution. Appropriate amendments would need to be made in Prevention of Corruption Act and Delhi Police Establishment Act for this purpose.	Agreed
The Lokpal Bill should provide for both - Lokpal at centre and Lokayuktas in states	Agreed

Experience shows that despite strong evidence against some judges, permission was denied by the Chief Justices. During the meeting, Prashant Bhushan reminded Mr Chidambaram, how Mr Chidambaram had sought permission to register an FIR against a judge of Kolkatta High Court but the permission was denied by the then Chief Justice of India. Subsequently when the said judge of Kolkatta High Court retired, he was raided and arrested the very next day, which means that the evidence against that judge was very strong. This shows that the present system of seeking permission from the Chief Justice of India has not worked and has ended up protecting the corrupt judges.

In Jan Lokpal Bill, it has been suggested that the permission should be granted by a seven member bench of Lokpal rather than the Chief Justice of India. A draft titled "basic principles of Jan Lokpal Bill" was submitted to the Joint Committee by the civil society representatives in second meeting of Joint committee held on 2nd May 2011.

First seven points of this document were discussed in the third meeting of the committee on 7th May. The rest of the 40 points were discussed on 23rd May.

On the basis of suggestions received in public consultations and on website, we had firmed up 31 suggestions, which were also submitted to the Joint Committee today. The same are attached on following table.

On the rest of the points, brief discussions took place, and the issue were postponed for further examination.

23rd May meeting was quite disastrous. It started with Anna demanding more frequent meetings as the progress had been quite slow till now. Anna also said that the government had been postponing discussions on even simple issues so far. This way, the meetings would continue indefinitely.

Broadly, the government disagreed on almost everything:

1. Government said - "Prime Minister should not be covered under Lokpal." We were shocked to hear that because

Issue	Government's response/decision
Powers of contempt to get its orders implemented and power to summon	Government agreed
It shall have the powers to recommend, on an annual basis, the number of special courts required under section 4 of Prevention of Corruption Act, to ensure that the trial in any case is completed in less than a year. The recommendations shall be binding on the government.	Government agreed that Lokpal may recommend but recommendation should not be binding. We asked them why it could not be made binding? We were told that it was due to three reasons: because Parliament may or may not agree to sanction expenditure, High Courts may not appoint judges and there could be lack of infrastructure. We said that we could examine how to overcome these issues but we would not agree to making it advisory.
Notify list of moveable and immoveable assets of accused, if during or at the time of conclusion of investigations, Lokpal believes that prosecution is likely to be initiated. These assets cannot be transferred after such notification. Loss to exchequer quantified at the time of conviction, could be recovered from sale of these assets.	Government agreed. But at what point should notification be issued, this would be decided after studying Bihar Special Courts Act. Also, some principles may be laid down on how the loss would be assessed by the court.
Recommend stay of any activity, if during investigations, Lokpal is satisfied that the allegations against such activity are likely to be sustained. If Government does not accept it within 30 days, Lokpal may get a stay order from HC against that activity.	In principle, government agreed. However, this needs to be appropriately formulated.

Direct transfer of any official, if his continuance is likely to adversely affect investigations.	Government agreed to make this power advisory. However, we are in favor of making it binding.
Powers to issue appropriate directions to prevent destruction of records during investigations, or to prevent the public servant from secreting the assets allegedly acquired by him through corrupt means.	Agreed
If the allegations against any minister are substantiated after any enquiry or investigations, then for non-criminal misconduct, Lokpal would submit its report to the President with its recommendations.	Agreed
Lokpal shall have powers to delegate any of its powers and functions barring those which are specifically to be performed by the benches of Lokpal.	There was a long discussion on this issue. Government's vision of Lokpal is an 11 member body, which will have quasi judicial powers and that body will pass all orders. That is very different from our vision. Such a model would create problems as that would overburden Lokpal with immense workload and make Lokpal unwieldy. Our vision of Lokpal - an institution headed by 11 member body. This body would have quasi judicial powers but primarily be a supervisory body. There will be many officers under that body, who would be designated authorities under this Act and would themselves also have quasi judicial powers under this Act. Government would examine it and revert.

Every complaint shall have to be compulsorily disposed by Lokpal. No complaint could be disposed without giving an opportunity of being hear to the complainant. If any case is closed, all records related thereto shall be made public.	Agreed
There shall be complete transparency during investigations also. However, such records, which could impede the process of investigations, would not be disclosed. But after the completion of any investigation or enquiry, all records related to a case, shall be made public.	Agreed
Lokpal shall publish, every month on its website, the status of cases, received, disposed, closed, reasons for closure and list of cases pending.	Agreed
Any complaint against a staff of Lokpal shall be enquired into within a month of its receipt and if found correct, the staff shall be summarily dismissed from the job. If any criminal case is made out, the same shall be pursued.	Agreed.
The minimum punishment shall be raised to one year of rigorous imprisonment and maximum should be raised to life imprisonment.	No agreement on life imprisonment
Punishment shall be higher if the status or rank of accused is higher.	No agreement

Lokpal shall be responsible for providing protection against professional or physical threat or victimization to whistleblowers, victims of corruption and witnesses whether within or outside the government.	Agreed in principle that Lokpal should be nodal agency. However, it would be examined at what stage is the pending whistleblower Bill of the government. It would be examined whether whistleblower protection should be provided in this Act or in the other Act. If it is provided in the other Act, that Act would also be discussed and finalized by this committee only.
If any asset is subsequently found to be owned by a public servant, which was not declared, it would be deemed to have been obtained through corrupt means unless he proves otherwise.	Agreed
If any asset is subsequently found to be in possession of any public servant, it shall be deemed to be owned by him/her unless he proves otherwise.	Agreed
After each elections, the Lokpal shall verify the assets declared by each candidate with his declared sources of income in his tax returns. Those undeclared shall be investigated against.	Only elected representatives and not all candidates. Agreed.
No rules shall be made without the approval of Lokpal. Lokpal shall have power to make rules and regulations with respect to its own functioning.	Agreed

All records of Lokpal shall be open barring the following: 1. Such portions of any records which if released during any ongoing investigations, could impede the process of investigations. However, after completion of investigations, they would be disclosed. 2. Such records which could affect national security or 3. Such records which would disclose the identity of a whistleblower and could compromise his/her security.	Agreed
If anyone makes a complaint which lacks any evidence or basis and is held by Lokpal to be meant only to harass someone, the complainant shall be fined. However, merely closure of a case due to lack of evidence shall not be held against a complainant.	Agreed

in the draft bill prepared by the government in January this year, PM was covered, though with some exceptions. Today, they wanted PM to be completely out of Lokpal's investigations. This was shocking for us. They said that if any enquiry starts against the PM, the PM would lose all authority to govern and take decisions. Prashant Bhushan reminded that in Bofors case also, the then PM was under scanner. But that did not deter him from taking decisions. Mr Chidambaram said that the PM's position would be weakened if there were allegations against him every other day. He was reminded that an unsubstantiated complaint would not be entertained. A seven member bench of Lokpal would first hear that complaint and decide whether there was an adequate prima facie evidence against the PM. If there were none, the complaint would be dismissed. However, government did not agree.

2. Government said - "Judiciary would be out of Lokpal." We reminded them that all that we were asking for was power to a seven member bench of Lokpal to decide whether an FIR should be registered against a judge or not. Today, only Chief Justice of India has the power to give that permission. And despite so much evidence against so many judges in public domain, permission had been given only in one case in the last 20 years. In the meeting held on 7th May, Prashant Bhushan had even told Mr Chidambaram how Mr Chidambaram himself had sought permission to register FIR against Justice Sen Gupta of Kolkatta High Court. Permission was sought from the then Chief Justice of India, Justice Venkatachaliah, who is very well known for his integrity. However, even Justice Venkatachaliah did not give permission. Was the evidence against Justice Sen Gupta strong enough? The strength of the evidence can be gauged from the fact that Justice Sen Gupta was raided and arrested soon after he retired because after retirement, permission of CJI was not required.

However, the government did not agree saying it would compromise the independence of judiciary. We said that the independence of judiciary was compromised under the present system which was encouraging corruption. Government said that judiciary should be dealt under Judicial Standards and Accountability Bill, which was pending in Parliament. We told them that the said Bill was very bad and would end up protecting corrupt judges rather than punishing them. Also, interestingly, the said Bill does not even talk of punishing and prosecuting "corruption" of judges. It only talks of enquiring against their "Misbehaviour". The government said that they would include corruption also in the said bill. Then we said, if you want to include judiciary's corruption in that bill, let this committee decide on drafting that Bill also. To that they refused. They said - you give your suggestions and we will recommend them to the Standing committee. This means that the government wants to include judiciary in a weak and ineffective Bill and does not want their corruption to be dealt through a strong and effective mechanism.

3. MPs bribery inside Parliament will not be covered - If a MP takes bribe to vote or ask questions in Parliament, which would not be covered under Lokpal. Only his conduct outside will be covered. What does an MP do outside Parliament? Just recommend projects out of his Constituency fund. There too, he merely recommends and the project is executed by the officers. Therefore, effectively, all MPs would be outside the purview of Lokpal. Purchase and sale of MPs is endangering the very foundations of our democracy. They may be purchased not just by other parties but could be purchased by other countries or corporates. Therefore, in order to save our democracy, it is extremely important that this is covered under Lokpal. However, the Government said that the Parliament should be allowed to do "self regulation". We told them that this self regulation had not worked and their corruption should be investigated by some independent body. They simply refused.

4. All officers will not be covered under Lokpal: Only Joint Secretary and above will be covered. Who will deal with corruption at levels below that? They said that the existing system would continue. But the existing system was not working. They had no answers. We said that the common man wants an answer to corruption in his day to day life -

bad roads, corruption in PDS etc. Who will deal with it? We said that the whole country had risen against corruption to seek solutions to corruption at all levels.

5. CBI, CVC and departmental vigilance will not be merged in Lokpal: Government said that let all these agencies continue. Let Lokpal have its own machinery. But why does the government want to keep a CBI under its own control? It appears that the Prime Minister does not want to be investigated by an independent body but will get himself investigated by CBI, which is directly under his own control. Also, CBI has been misused by every successive government to arm twist politically inconvenient opponents. Government perhaps wants to continue doing that.

6. Public Grievances: Government agreed to the concept of citizens charter and that violation of citizens charter would be deemed to be corruption at some stage of upscaling of a grievance.

Justice Santosh Hegde asked the government - "Then who is covered under Lokpal? And what is the purpose of creating such a Lokpal?"

Effectively, the Lokpal would have jurisdiction only on Joint Secretary and above officers but not on PM. There would be around 2000 such odd officers in Government of India. Are we creating Lokpal for investigating corruption of such a few officers? Was this the purpose of such a big anti-corruption movement in India?

Definitely government's intentions are suspect. Please prepare yourself for the next huge movement in the country. We will go to government meetings in the next few meetings. We will try our best, till the last moment, to persuade the government to agree to a strong and effective Lokpal Bill. But if the government disagrees, we should be ready for taking to streets.

What are Lokpal and Lokayukta?

Why are Lokpal and Lokayukta needed?

How will Lokpal and Lokayukta be different from the

prevalent system of fighting corruption?

We propose that there should be established a 'Lokpal' at the central level and 'Lokayukta' at the state level, both of which will address the inadequacies of the current anti-corruption systems and have the power and independence to investigate and prosecute cases of corruption.

To be established through the enactment of central and state-level laws, Lokpal and Lokayukta will work on behalf of the citizens of India to protect their interests from abuse of public office at the level of the central and state governments, respectively.

These 'people's commissions' will be independent of the government in a manner that politicians and bureaucrats are not able to interfere in their functioning. They will be accountable to the citizens through transparency in their selection and functioning. Lokpal and Lokayukta will also be made accountable to the citizens by giving the latter the right to file complaints against the former at the Supreme Court and the High Court, respectively.

Lokpal and Lokayukta will protect citizens who show the courage to bring to the notice of the authorities any instance of abuse of public office. The people's commissions will also deal with certain kinds of grievances reported by the citizens in respect of any service or office of the central and state governments and provide them redress.

The establishment of Lokpal and Lokayukta will do away with multiplicity of anti-corruption agencies; each of these people's commissions will have 10 members and one chairperson.

Other Features

1. Upon non-compliance with its orders, the Lokpal or Lokayukta will have the powers to impose financial penalties and also initiate contempt proceedings against the guilty officials.

	CURRENT SYSTEM	PROPOSED LOKPAL-LOKAYUKTA SYSTEM
Functioning of lokpal	Ordinary citizens complaining against corruption have little trust in the prevailing anti-corruption systems because they believe they will not be listened to or nothing will come out of the registration of their complaints. In the prevailing systems, there is no time limit within which a complaint against corruption is to be investigated. Often, the anti-corruption agencies just close a case without informing the complainant. The investigation into corruption may also turn corrupt, such as when the anti-corruption agencies accept bribes to close a case.	Any ordinary citizen can approach Lokpal and Lokayukta with any complaint of corruption. Lokpal or Lokayukta will have to complete its enquiries or investigations within one year. After investigation, if there is evidence of corruption found against a politician or any official, Lokpal or Lokayukta will have to file a case in appropriate trial court. The trial court will have to complete the trial and announce punishment within a year. Lokpal and Lokayukta will have the powers to get a guilty official dismissed or suspended. They will also have the powers to get an increment of a guilty official withheld or get a guilty official reduced in rank.
		The Lokpal or Lokayukta will make an annual estimate of the number of special courts required to ensure that the trial in each case is completed within a year. The government will have to set up such number of courts within three months of the Lokpal and Lokayukta making the request. Every complaint shall have to be compulsorily disposed by Lokpal or Lokayukta. No complaint could be disposed of without giving a hearing to the complainant. If any case is closed, all records related thereto shall be made public.

Judges - SC & HC	No FIR can be registered against any Supreme Court or High Court judge without the permission of Chief Justice of India. It has been seen in the past that the Chief Justice of India tries to protect his own brother judges and rarely gives such a permission.	Under Jan Lokpal Bill, the full bench of Lokpal will give permission to file a case against any judge. No permission will be required from Chief Justice of India.
Property attachment	In the current anti-corruption systems, there is no provision for attaching the properties of the persons being investigated.	Lokpal or Lokayukta will have the powers to notify the list of moveable and immoveable assets of the accused to be attached if, during investigations, the people's commissions come to believe that prosecution is likely to be initiated. These assets cannot be transferred after such notification. Loss to exchequer quantified at the time of conviction could be recovered from the sale of these assets.
Recovery of losses	Currently, there is no provision in our law to recover the public funds that have been misappropriated or make up for the loss to the exchequer on account of corrupt practices.	At the time of conviction, the court will make an assessment of the loss caused by the accused, which shall be recovered from them. If the beneficiary of the corrupt practices is a business entity, five times the loss caused to the government will be recovered. The recovery may be done from the assets of that business entity or the personal assets of its directors.
Punishment	The quantum of punishment for people convicted of corrupt practices range from six months to seven years of imprisonment, which is inadequate.	The punishment will range from one year to life imprisonment and will be commensurate with the status or rank of the accused. The quantum of punishment will be higher for a convict who had a higher rank than for a convict with the lower rank.

Ministers	In the current system, ministers continue in their positions despite substantial evidence against them.	If the allegations against a minister are substantiated through an enquiry or investigation, the Lokpal or Lokayukta will be able to recommend removal of that minister (other than the Prime Minister).
Evidence	In the current system, it is difficult to gather evidence of illegal obtainment of a public benefit on payment of bribe.	If a person obtains any benefit from the government in violation of a law or rules and regulations, that person along with concerned public servants shall be deemed to have indulged in corrupt practices.
Whistleblower protection	Currently, people who report corrupt practices or raise their voice against corruption are being threatened, victimized and even murdered. There is no protection for them.	Lokpal and Lokayukta will be responsible for providing the whistleblowers, inside or outside the government, with protection from a threat or victimization of a professional or physical kind.
Citizen's charter	Currently, it is easy for a corrupt public official to compel a citizen to pay a bribe by simply refusing to do the work without a bribe. The citizen's choice is limited to paying a bribe to get the work done or not paying a bribe and not getting the work done.	Every department shall prepare a citizens charter listing all the routine and easily definable works along with the official responsible for a particular work and the time frame in which the work will be done. Each department will also designate its head or a sufficiently senior officer as public grievance officer (PGO). A complaint of non-adherence to the citizen's charter will be dealt by the PGO, who will be required to get the work done in 30 days.

		If the PGO fails to provide redress, the grievance will go to the vigilance officer (who will be a part of the Lokpal) and the grievance will be deemed to have a vigilance officer. The vigilance officer will get the work done in the next 30 days, impose penalties on the erring officials which will be paid as compensation to the citizen and proceed with enquiries of misconduct against the erring officials.
Multiplicity of A.C. agencies	Currently, there are multiple anti- corruption agencies that are ineffective on their own and together. These multiple agencies often waste their effort on the same case or work at cross purposes. The net result is a very weak check on corruption and the corrupt.	All existing anti-corruption agencies will be merged into Lokpal. The anti-corruption wing of CBI, the CVC and the vigilance wings of all departments will be merged into Lokpal.

2. Each bureaucrat, politician and judge would be required to submit his/her statement of moveable and immoveable assets on an annual basis, which will be put on the official website. If an asset of substantial value is subsequently found to be owned by a public servant, it would be deemed to have been obtained through corrupt means.
3. After each election, the Lokpal will verify the assets declared by each candidate from his/her declared sources of income in his/her tax returns. If undeclared assets are found, they will become the subject of investigation.
4. All records of Lokpal will be open barring the following:
   a. Such portions of any records which, if released during any ongoing investigation, could impede the process of investigation. However, after completion of investigation, they would be disclosed.
   b. Such records which could affect national security or
   c. Such records which would disclose the identity of a whistleblower and could compromise his/her security.
5. Lokpal will publish every month on its website the status of cases received, disposed, closed, reasons for closure and the list of cases pending.
6. So that the government may not be influence their functioning or they may not get aligned to any political party, the Chairperson and members will not be eligible for appointment to any position in the government or for contesting elections after they leave office.
7. Selection of members and Chairperson of Lokpal and Lokayukta:
   a) The ten members and the chairperson of Lokpal

are appointed by a *Selection Committee* that comprises of the Prime Minister, Leader of the opposition in Lok Sabha, two youngest judges of Supreme Court (SC), two youngest Chief Justices of High Courts, Comptroller and Auditor General (CAG), Chief Election Commissioner (CEC) and the immediately outgoing members of Lokpal.

b) The *Selection Committee* makes the above appointment from a pool of shortlisted candidates that has been identified by a *"Search Committee"*.

c) The *"Search Committee"* is a 10-member committee formed as follows. First, the *Selection Committee* selects five members from ex-CECs and ex-CAGs who have unimpeachable integrity, no connection with government or political parties. These five members then select another five members from the civil society. This completes the 10-member *SearchCommittee.*

d) The *Search Committee* will choose from the people of India, three times the number of vacancies to be filled for the position of Lokpal member and chairperson. Such selection will be based on strict criteria to filter out people with any doubtful integrity or connections with any government body or political party. This list is then forwarded to the *Selection Committee* which then makes the selection from this pool.

e) After the selection, the names are forwarded to the President of India, who will then immediately appoint the recommended Lokpal members.

f) The entire process of selection of Lokpal is publicly transparent via website. All the meetings of the *Search Committee* and *Selection Committee* shall be video recorded that will be made public.

8. Removal of members and Chairperson of Lokpal and Lokayukta:

   Lokpal members and/or chairperson may be removed on misconduct or corruption charges only by a ruling of a bench of the Supreme Court (SC) comprising of the 5 senior-most judges. Any person may move a petition before the SC seeking such removal. After hearing the matter, SC may order the formation of a Special Investigation Team that will conduct an inquiry and submit a report within 3 months, and/or order the withdrawal of partial or complete work from that Lokpal member.

5

Corruption in India

Political and bureaucratic corruption in India are major concerns. A 2005 study conducted by Transparency International in India found that more than 45% of Indians had first-hand experience of paying bribes or influence peddling to get jobs done in public offices successfully.

Transparency International estimates that truckers pay US$5 billion in bribes annually. In 2010 India was ranked 87th out of 178 countries in Transparency International's Corruption Perceptions Index.

Overview

Although former Prime Minister and Congress party leader Indira Gandhi is quoted as saying that corruption is a misuse of power, she also publicly stated "nonchalantly" that "corruption was a global phenomenon" and her government was no different. Successive central governments and members of India's famous Nehru-Gandhi political dynasty have often been accused most of corruption and amassing illegal wealth among India's political class. The year 2011 has proved to be a watershed in the public tolerance of political corruption in India, with widespread public protests and movements led by social activists against corruption and for the return of illegal wealth stashed by politicians and businessmen in foreign banks over the six decades since independence.

Criminalization is also a serious problem in contemporary Indian politics. In July 2008, The Washington Post reported that nearly a fourth of the 540 Indian Parliament members faced criminal charges, "including human trafficking, immigration rackets, embezzlement, rape and even murder".

India tops the list for black money in the entire world with almost US$1456 billion in Swiss banks (approximately USD 1.4 trillion) in the form of black money. According to the data provided by the Swiss Banking Association Report (2006), India has more black money than the rest of the world combined. To put things in perspective, Indian-owned Swiss bank account assets are worth 13 times the country's national debt.

Independent reports published through 1991 to 2011 calculated the financial net worth of India's most powerful and traditionally ruling family (the Nehru-Gandhi political dynasty) to be anywhere between $9.41 billion (Rs 42,345 crore) to $18.66 billion (Rs 83,900 crore), most of it in the form of illegal monies. Harvard scholar Yevgenia Albats cited KGB correspondence about payments to Rajiv Gandhi and his family, which had been arranged by Viktor Chebrikov, which shows that KGB chief Viktor Chebrikov sought in writing an "authorization to make payments in US dollars to the family members of Rajiv Gandhi, namely Sonia Gandhi, Rahul Gandhi and Paola Maino, mother of Sonia Gandhi" from the CPSU in December 1985.

"The recent scams involving unimaginably big amounts of money, such as the 2G spectrum scam, are well known. It is estimated that more than trillion dollars are stashed away in foreign havens, while 80% of Indians earn less than $2 per day and every second child is malnourished. It seems as if only the honest people are poor in India and want to get rid of their poverty by education, emigration to cities, and immigration, whereas all the corrupt ones, like Hasan Ali Khan are getting rich through scams and crime. It seems as if India is a rich country filled with poor people", the organisers of Dandi March II in the United States said.

The Comptroller and Auditor General of India said, "As on March 31, 2010, unutilised committed external assistance was of the order of Rs.1,05,339 crore."

History

The economy of India was under socialist-inspired policies for an entire generation from the 1950s until the late 1980s. The economy was subject to extensive regulation, protectionism, and public ownership, leading to pervasive corruption and slow growth. License Raj was often at the core of corruption.

The Vohra Report, submitted by the former Indian Union Home Secretary, N.N. Vohra, in October 1993, studied the problem of the criminalisation of politics and of the nexus among criminals, politicians and bureaucrats in India.

Independent reports published through 1991 to 2011 calculated the financial net worth of India's most powerful and traditionally ruling family (Nehru Gandhi Political Dynasty) to be anywhere between $9.41 billion (Rs 42,345 crore) to $18.66 billion (Rs 83,900 crore), most of it in the form of illegal monies. Harvard scholar Yevgenia Alaan cited KGB correspondence about payments to Rajiv Gandhi and his family, which had been arranged by Viktor Chebrikov, which shows that KGB chief Viktor Chebrikov sought in writing an "authorization to make payments in US dollars to the family members of Rajiv Gandhi, namely Sonia Gandhi, Rahul Gandhi and Paola Maino, mother of Sonia Gandhi" from the CPSU in December 1985.

The report contained several observations made by official agencies on the criminal network which was virtually running a parallel government. It also discussed criminal gangs who enjoyed the patronage of politicians of all political parties and the protection of government functionaries. It revealed that political leaders had become the leaders of gangs. They were connected to the military. Over the years criminals had been elected to local bodies, State Assemblies, and even the Parliament. The unpublished annexures to the Vohra Report are believed to contain highly explosive material.

According to Jitendra Singh, "in the bad old days, particularly pre-1991, when the License Raj held sway, and by design, all kinds of free market mechanisms were hobbled or stymied, and corruption emerged almost as an illegitimate price mechanism, a shadowy quasi-market, such that scarce resources could still be allocated within the economy, and decisions could get made. These were largely distortions created by the politico-economic regime. While a sea change has occurred in the years following 1991, some of the distorted cultural norms that took hold during the earlier period are slowly being repaired by the sheer forces of competition. The process will be long and slow, however. It will not change overnight." One of the major problems and obstacles to development that many developing countries face is corruption by greedy, power-hungry politicians, which is endemic in certain parts of the world.

Politics

As of December 2008, 120 of India's 522 parliament members were facing criminal charges. Many of the biggest scandals since 2010 have involved very high levels of government, including Cabinet Ministers and Chief Ministers, such as in the 2G spectrum scam and the Adarsh Housing Society Scam.

Bureaucracy

A 2005 study done by Transparency International (TI) in India found that more than 50% of the people had firsthand experience of paying bribe or peddling influence to get a job done in a public office. Taxes and bribes are common between state borders; Transparency International estimates that truckers pay annually US$5 billion in bribes. A 2009 survey of the leading economies of Asia, revealed Indian bureaucracy to be not just least efficient out of Singapore, Hong Kong, Thailand, South Korea, Japan, Malaysia, Taiwan, Vietnam, China, Philippines and Indonesia; further it was also found that working with India's civil servants was a "slow and painful" process.

Land and Property

Officials often steal state property. In cities and villages throughout India, Mafia Raj consisting of municipal and other government officials, elected politicians, judicial officers, real estate developers and law enforcement officials, acquire, develop and sell land in illegal ways.

Tendering Processes and Awarding Contracts

Government officials having discretionary powers in awarding contracts engage in preferential treatment for selected bidders and display negligence in quality control processes. Many state-funded construction activities in India, such as road building, are dominated by construction mafias, which are groupings of corrupt public works officials, materials suppliers, politicians and construction contractors. Shoddy construction and material substitution (e.g. mixing sand in cement while submitting expenses for cement) result in roads and highways being dangerous, and sometimes simply washed away when India's heavy monsoon season arrives.

Medicine

In Government Hospitals, corruption is associated with non availability of medicines (or duplicate/fake medicines), getting admission, consultations with doctors and availing diagnostic services. There have been cases of diversion of medical supplies from government hospitals and clinics as well as supply and distribution of medicines of inferior quality.

Income tax Department

There have been several cases of collusion of officials of the income tax department of India for a favorable tax treatment in return for bribes.

Preferential Award of Public Resources

Land in areas with short supply is relatively common with government entities awarding public land to private concerns at negligible rates. Other examples include the award of mining leases to private companies without a levy of taxes that is proportionate to the market value of the ore.

Judiciary

According to Transparency International, judicial corruption in India is attributable to factors such as "delays in the disposal of cases, shortage of judges and complex procedures, all of which are exacerbated by a preponderance of new laws".

Armed Forces

The Indian Armed Forces have frequently witnessed corruption involving senior armed forces officers from the Indian Army, Indian Navy and Indian Air Force. Many officers have been caught for allegedly selling defence stores in the black market in the border districts of Indian states and territories. Recent sukhna land scandal involving four Indian Lieutenant Generals has shaken public faith in the country's growing military at a time when large sums are being spent on modernising the armed forces. A string of eye-popping fraud cases has damaged the institution in recent years. The latest Adarsh land scam is another example of the nexus between the armed forces, bureaucracy and the politicians in the embezzlement of government property.

Religious Institutions

In India, the corruption has also crept into religious institutions. Some of the Church of North India are making money by selling Baptism certificates. A group of church leaders and activists has launched a campaign to combat the corruption within churches. The chief economic consequences of corruption are the loss to the economy, an unhealthy climate for investment and an increase in the cost of government-subsidised services. The TI India study estimates the monetary value of petty corruption in 11 basic services provided by the government, like education, healthcare, judiciary, police, etc., to be around ₹ 21,068 crore (US$4.7 billion). India still ranks in the bottom quartile of developing nations in terms of the ease of doing business, and compared to China and other lower developed Asian nations, the average time taken to secure the clearances for a startup or to invoke bankruptcy is much greater.

Right to Information Act

The Right to Information Act (2005) and equivalent acts in the states, that require government officials to furnish information requested by citizens or face punitive action, computerization of services and various central and state government acts that established vigilance commissions have considerably reduced corruption or at least have opened up avenues to redress grievances. The 2006 report by Transparency International puts India at the 70th place and states that significant improvements were made by India in reducing corruption.

Ombudsmen

The Lokayukta is an anti-government corruption organization in the Indian states. These institutions are based on the Ombudsman in Scandinavian countries. An amendment to the

Constitution has been proposed to implement the Lokayukta uniformly across Indian States as a three-member body, headed by a retired Supreme Court judge or high court chief justice, and comprise of the state vigilance commissioner and a jurist or an eminent administrator as other members.

Social welfare worker Anna Hazare has led a movement to compel the Indian Government to notify the Committee for the implementation of the Lokayukta against corruption as an independent body and also giving enough powers to the Lokayukta to also receive corruption complaints against politicians, bureaucrats and even sitting judges. Anna Hazare is currently pursuing an agenda to pass a bill called Jan Lokpal bill, and he has gathered the support of many citizens residing in metropolitan cities of India. He is currently on an indefinite fast at the Ramlila Grounds, Delhi, in order to campaign for the cause.

Whistleblowers

Whistleblowers play a major role in the fight against corruption. India currently does not have a law to protect whistleblowers, which was highlighted by the assassination of Satyendra Dubey. Indian courts are regularly ordering probe in cases of murders or so-called suicide of several whistle blowers. One of the latest case of such murder is of V Sasindran Company Secretary of Palakkad based Malabar Cement Limited, a Government company in Kerala and his two minor children, Kerala High Court ordered CBI probe on 18 February 2011. Initially, CBI showed its unwillingness for probing into such cases citing over-burden as a reason.

Anti-corruption Police and Courts

The income tax department of India, Central Vigilance Commission and Central Bureau of Investigation all deal with anti-corruption initiatives.

There have been calls for the Indian government to create

an anti-theft law enforcement agency that investigates and prosecutes corruption in government at national, state and local levels. Special courts that are more efficient than the traditional Indian courts with traveling judges and law enforcement agents are being proposed. The proposal has not yet been acted upon by the Indian government. Certain states such as Andhra Pradesh (Andhra Pradesh Anti-corruption Bureau) and Karnataka (Lokayukta) have similar agencies and courts.

Anti-corruption Organizations

A variety of organizations have been created in India to actively fight against corrupt government and business practices. Notable organizations include:

- 5th Pillar is most known for the creation of the zero rupee note, a valueless note designed to be given to corrupt officials when they request bribes.
- India Against Corruption is a movement created by a citizens from a variety of professions and statuses to work against corruption in India. It is currently headed by Anna Hazare.

Jaago Re! One Billion Votes is an organization originally founded by Tata Tea and Janaagraha to increase youth voter registration. They have since expanded their work to include other social issues, including corruption.

Association for Social Transparency, Rights And Action (ASTRA) is an NGO focused on grass-roots work to fight corruption in Karnataka.

One organization, the Lok Satta Movement, has transformed itself from a civil organization to a full-fledged political party, the Lok Satta Party. The party has fielded candidates in Andhra Pradesh, Tamil Nadu, and Bangalore. In 2008, it obtained its first elected post, when Jayaprakash Narayan won the election for the Kukatpally Assembly Constituency in Andrha Pradesh.

Effects of Corruption

According to a report by KPMG, "high-level corruption and scams are now threatening to derail the country's credibility and its economic boom".

THE PREVENTION OF CORRUPTION ACT, 1988

(Central Act No.49 of 1988)

(9th September 1988)

An Act to consolidate and amend the law relating to the Prevention of Corruption and for matters connected therewith.

Be it enacted by the Parliament in the Thirty-ninth Year of the Republic of India as follows:-

CHAPTER - I : PRELIMINARY

1. Short title and extent.

(1) This Act may be called the Prevention of Corruption Act, 1988.

(2) It extends to the whole of India except the State of Jammu & Kashmir and it applies also to all Citizens of India outside India.

2. Definitions. In this Act, unless the context otherwise requires.-

(a) "Election" means any election, by whatever means held under any law for the purpose of selecting members of Parliament or any Legislature, local authority or other public authority;

(b) "Public Duty" means a duty in the discharge of which the State, the public or the community at large has an interest;

Explanation: In this clause "State" includes a Corporation established by or under a Central,

Provincial or State Act, or an authority or a body owned or controlled or aided by the Government or a Government company as defined in Section 617 of the Companies Act, 1956 (1 of 1956);

(c) "Public Servant" means.-

(i) any person in the service or pay of the Government or remunerated by the Government by fees or commission for the performance of any public duty;

(ii) any person in the service or pay of a local authority;

(iii) any person in the service or pay of a Corporation established by or under a Central, Provincial or State Act, or an authority or a body owned or controlled or aided by the Government or a Government Company as defined in Section 617 of the Companies Act, 1956 (1 of 1956)

(iv) any judge, including any person empowered by Law to discharge, whether by himself or as a member of anybody of persons, any adjudicatory functions;

(v) any person authorized by a court of justice to perform any duty, in connection with the administration of justice, including a liquidator, receiver or commissioner appointed by such court.

(vi) any arbitrator or other person to whom, any cause or matter has been referred for decision or report by a court of justice or by a competent public authority.

(vii) any person who holds an office by virtue of which he is empowered to prepare, publish, maintain or revise an electoral roll or to conduct an election or part of an election;

(viii) any person who holds an office by virtue of which he is authorised or required to perform any public duty;

(ix) any person who is the president, Secretary or of other office bearer of a registered co-operative society engaged in agriculture, industry, trade or banking, receiving or having received any financial aid from the Central Government or a State Government or from any Corporation established by or under a Central, Provincial or State Act, or any authority or body owned or controlled or aided by the Government or a Government Company as defined in Section 617 of the Companies Act, 1956 (1 of 1956);

(x) any person who is a Chairman, member or employee of any Service Commission or Board, by whatever name called, or a member of any selection committee appointed by such Commission or Board for the conduct of any examination or making any selection on behalf of such Commission or Board;

(xi) any person who is a Vice-Chancellor or member of any governing body, professor, reader, lecturer or any other teacher or employee, by whatever designation called, of any University and any person whose services have been availed of by a University or any other public authority in connection with holding or conducting examinations;

(xii) any person who is an office bearer or an employee of an educational, scientific, social, cultural or other institution, in whatever manner established, receiving or having received any financial assistance from the Central Government or any State Government or local or other public authority.

Explanation 1: persons falling under any of the above sub-clauses or public servants whether appointed by the Government or not.

Explanation 2: Wherever the words "Public Servant" occur, they shall be understood of every person who is in actual possession of the situation of a public servant, Whatever legal defect there may be in his right to hold that situation.

CHAPTER - II : APPOINTMENT OF SPECIAL JUDGES

3. Power to appoint Special Judges.

(1) The Central Government or the State Government may, by Notification in the Official Gazette appoint as many special judges as may be necessary for such area or areas or for such a case or group of cases as may be specified in the notification to try the following offences, namely.-

(a) any offence punishable under this Act, and

(b) any conspiracy to commit or any attempt to commit or any abetment of any of the offences specified in clause(a).

(2) A person shall not be qualified for appointment as a Special Judge under this Act unless he is or has been a Sessions Judge or an additional Sessions Judge or an assistant Sessions Judge under the Code of Criminal Procedure, 1973(2 of 1974)

4. Cases triable by Special Judges.

(1) Notwithstanding anything contained in the Code of Criminal Procedure 1973 (2 of 1974) or in any other Law for the time being in force, the offences

specified in sub-section (1) of Section 3 shall be tried by the Special Judges only.

(2) Every offence specified in sub-section (1) of Section 3 shall be tried by the Special Judge for the area within which it was committed, or as the case may be, by the Special Judge appointed for the case, or where there are no special judges than one for such area, by such one of them as may be specified in this behalf by the Central Government.

(3) When trying any case, a Special Judge may also try an offence, other than an offence specified in Section 3, with which the accused may, under the Code of Criminal Procedure, 1973 (2 of 1974), be charged at the same trial.

(4) Notwithstanding anything contained in the Code of Criminal Procedure, 1973 (2 of 1974), a Special Judge shall, as far as practicable, hold the trial of an offence on day-to-day basis.

5. Procedure and Powers of Special Judge.

(1) A Special Judge may take cognizance of offences without the accused being committed to him for trial and, in trying the accused person, shall follow procedure prescribed by the Code of Criminal Procedure, 1973(2 of 1974), for the trial of Warrant cases by the Magistrates.

(2) A Special Judge may, with a view to obtaining the evidence of any person supposed to have been directly or indirectly concerned in, or privy to an offence, tender a pardon to such person on condition of his making a full and true disclosure of the whole circumstances within his knowledge relating to the offence and to every other person, concerned, whether as Principal or abettor, in the commission there of and any pardon so tendered

shall, for the purposes of sub-sections (1) to (5) of Section 308 of the Code of Criminal Procedure, 1973 (2 of 1974), be deemed to have been tendered under Section 307 of that Code.

(3) Save as provided in sub/section (1) or sub-section (2), the provisions of the Code of Criminal Procedure 1973(2 of 1974), shall, so far as they are not inconsistent with this Act applied to the proceedings before a Special Judge and for the purposes of the said provisions, the court of the Special Judge shall be deemed to be a Court of Sessions and the persons conducting a prosecution before Special Judge shall be deemed to be a public prosecutor.

(4) In particular and without prejudice to the generality of the provisions contained in sub-section (3), the provisions of sections 326 and 475 of the Code of Criminal Procedure, 1973 (2 of 1974, shall so far as may be, applied to the proceeding before a special judge and for the purposes of the said provisions, a Special Judge shall be deemed to be a Magistrate.

(5) A Special Judge may pass upon any person convicted by him any sentence authorized by law for the punishment of the offence of which such person is convicted.

(6) A Special Judge, while trying an offence punishable under this Act, shall exercise all the powers and functions exercisable by a District Judge under the Criminal Law Amendment Ordinance, 1944(Ordinance-38 of 1944).

6. Power to try Summarily.

(1) Where a Special Judge tries any offence specified in sub-section (1) of Section 3, alleged to have been committed by a Public Servant in relation to the contravention of any special order referred

to in sub-section (1) of Section 12-A of the Essential Commodities Act 1955(10 of 1955), or of an order referred to in clause(a) of sub-section (2) of that Section, than, notwithstanding anything containing in sub-section (1) of Section -5 of this Act or Section 260 of the Code of Criminal Procedure, 1973(2 of 1974) the Special Judge shall tray the offence in a summary way, and the provisions of sections 262 to 265 (both inclusive) of the said Code shall as far as may be, apply to such trial.

Provided that, in the case of any conviction in a summary trial under this section, it shall be lawful for the Special Judge to pass a Sentence of imprisonment for a term not exceeding one year:

Provided further that when at the commencement of, or in the course of, a summary trial under this Section, it appears to the Special Judge that the nature of the case is such that a sentence of imprisonment for a term exceeding one year may have to be passed or that it is, for any other reason, undesirable to try the case summarily, the Special Judge shall, after hearing the parties, record an order to that effect and thereafter, recall any witnesses who may have been examined and proceed to hear or rehear the case in accordance with the procedure prescribed by the said Code for the trial of warrant cases by Magistrates.

(2) Notwithstanding anything to the contrary contained in this Act or in the Code of Criminal Procedure, 1973 (2 of 1974), there shall be no appeal by a convicted person in any case tried summarily under this section in which the Special Judge passes a sentence of imprisonment not exceeding one month, and of fine not exceeding two thousand rupees whether or not any order under Section 452 of the said Code is made in addition to such sentence, but as appeal shall lie where

any sentence in excess of the aforesaid limits is passed by the Special Judge.

CHAPTER - III : OFFENCES AND PENALTIES

7. Public Servant taking gratification other than legal remuneration in respect of an official act. Whoever, being, or expecting to be a public servant accepts or obtains or agrees, to accept or attempts to obtain from any person, for himself or for any other person, any gratification whatever, other than legal remuneration as a motive or reward for doing or forbearing to do any official act or for showing or forbearing to show, in the exercise of his official functions, favour or disfavour to any person or for rendering or attempting to render any service or dis-service to any person, with the Central Government or any State Government or Parliament or the Legislature of any State or with any local authority, corporation or Government Company referred to in clause (c) of Section-2, or with any public servant, whether named or otherwise, shall be punishable with imprisonment which shall be not less than 6 months but which may extend to 5 years and shall also be liable to fine.

Explanations:

(a) "Expecting to be a public servant". If a person not expecting to be in office obtains a gratification by deceiving others into a belief that he is about to be in office and that he will then serve them, he may be guilty of cheating, but he is not guilty of the offence defined in this section.

(b) "Gratification". The word "gratification" is not restricted to pecuniary gratifications or to gratifications estimable in money.

(c) "Legal remuneration". The words "Legal remuneration" are not restricted to remuneration which a public servant can lawfully demand, but include all remuneration which he is permitted by the Government or the Organization, which he serves, to accept.

(d) "A motive or reward for doing". A person who receives a gratification as a motive or reward for doing what he does not intend or he is not in a position to do, or has not done, comes within this expression.

(e) Where a Public Servant induces a person erroneously to believe that his influence with the Government has obtained a title for that person and thus induces that person to give the public servant, money or any other gratification as a reward for this service, the public servant has committed an offence under this section.

8. Taking gratification, in order, by corrupt or illegal means, to influence public servant. Whoever accepts or obtains, or agrees to accept, or attempts to obtain, from any person, for himself or for any other person, any gratification whatever as a motive or reward for inducing, by corrupt or illegal means, any public servant, whether named or otherwise, to do or forbear to do any official act, or in the exercise of the official functions of such public servant to show favour or disfavour to any person, or to render or attempt to render any service or dis-service to any person with the Central Government or any State Government or Parliament or the Legislature of any State or with any local authority, corporation or Government, Company referred to in clause (c) of Section-2, or with any public servant, whether named or otherwise, shall be punishable with imprisonment for a term which shall be not less than six months but which may extend to five years and shall also be liable to fine.

9. Taking gratification, for exercise of personal influence with public servant. Whoever accepts or obtains, or agrees to accept, or attempts to obtain from any person, for himself or for any other person, any gratification whatever, as a motive or reward for inducing, by the exercise of personal influence, any public servant whether named or otherwise to do or to forbear to do any official act, or in the exercise of the official functions of such public servant to show favour or disfavour to any person, or to render or attempt to render any service or disservice to any person with the Central Government or any State Government or Parliament or the Legislature of any State or with any local authority, corporation or Government company referred to in clause (c) of Section 2, or with any public servant, whether named or otherwise, shall be punishable with imprisonment for a term which shall be not less than six months but which may extend to five years and shall also be liable to fine.

10. Punishment for abetment by public servant of offences defined in Section 8 or 9. Whoever, being a public servant, in respect of whom, either of the offences defined in Section 8 or Section 9 is committed, abets the offence, whether or not that offence is committed in consequence of that abetment shall be punishable with imprisonment for a term which shall be not less than six months but which may extend to five years and shall also be liable to fine.

11. Public servant obtaining valuable thing without consideration from person concerned in proceeding or business transacted by such public servant. Whoever, being a public servant, accepts or obtains or agrees to accept or attempts to obtain for himself, or for any other person, any valuable thing without consideration, or for a consideration which he knows to be inadequate, from any person whom he knows to have been or to be, or to be likely to be concerned in any proceeding or business transacted, or about to be transacted by such public servant, or having any connection with the official functions of himself or of any public servant to whom he is subordinate, or from any person whom he knows to be interested in or related to the person so concerned, shall be punishable with imprisonment for a term which shall be not less than six months but which may extend to five years and shall also be liable to fine.

12. Punishment for abetment of offences defined in Section 7 or 11. Whoever abets any offence punishable under Section 7 or Section 11 whether or not that offence is committed in consequence of that abetment, shall be punishable with imprisonment for a term which shall be not less than six months but which may extend to five years and shall also be liable to fine.

13. Criminal misconduct by a public servant.

(1) A public servant is said to commit the offence of criminal misconduct.-

(a) if he habitually accepts or obtains or agrees to accept or attempts to obtain from any person for himself or for any other person any gratification other than legal remuneration as a motive or reward such as is mentioned in Section 7; or

(b) if he habitually accepts or obtains or agrees to accept or attempts to obtain from any person for himself or for any other person, any valuable thing without consideration or for a consideration which he knows to be inadequate from any person whom he knows to have been, or to be likely to be concerned in any proceeding or business transacted or about to be transacted by him, or having any connection with the official functions of himself or of any public servant to whom he is subordinate, or from any person whom he knows to be interested in or related to the person so concerned; or

(c) if he dishonestly or fraudulently misappropriates or otherwise converts for his own use any property entrusted to him or under his control as a public servant or allows any other person so to do ; or

(d) if he.-

(i) by corrupt or illegal means, obtains for himself or for any other person any valuable thing or pecuniary advantage; or

(ii) by abusing his position as a public servant, obtains for himself or for any other person any valuable thing or pecuniary advantage; or

(iii) while holding office as a public servant obtains for any person any valuable thing or pecuniary advantage without any public interest ; or

(e) if he or any person on his behalf, is in possession or has, at any time during the period of his office, been in possession for which the public servant cannot satisfactorily account, of pecuniary resources or property disproportionate to his known sources of income.

Explanation: For the purposes of this section, "known sources of income" means income received from any lawful source and such receipt has been intimated in accordance with the provisions of any law, rules or orders for the time being applicable to a public servant.

(2) Any public servant, who commits criminal misconduct shall be punishable with imprisonment for a term which shall be not less than one year but which may extend to 7 years and shall also be liable to fine.

14. Habitual committing of offence under Section 8, 9 and 12. Whoever habitually commits.-

(a) an offence punishable under Section 8 or Section 9 ; or

office.

(2) Where for any reason whatsoever any doubt arises as to whether the previous sanction as required under sub-section (1) should be given by the Central Government or the State Government or any other authority, such sanction shall be given by that Government or authority which would have been competent to remove the public servant from his office at the time when the offence was alleged to have been committed.

(3) Notwithstanding anything contained in the Code of Criminal Procedure, 1973 (2 of 1974).-

(a) no finding, sentence or order passed by a Special Judge shall be reversed or altered by a Court in appeal, confirmation or revision on the ground of the absence of, or any error, omissions or irregularity in, the sanction required under sub-section (1), unless, in the opinion of that Court, a failure of Justice has in fact been occasioned thereby .

(b) no court shall stay the proceedings under this Act on the ground of any error, omission or irregularity in the sanction granted by the authority, unless it is satisfied that such error, omission, or irregularity has resulted in a failure of justice;

(c) no Court shall stay the proceedings under this Act on any other ground and no Court shall exercise the powers of revision in relation to any interlocutory order passed in any inquiry, trial, appeal or other proceedings.

(4) In determining under sub-section (3) whether the absence of, or any error, omission or irregularity in, such sanction as occasioned or resulted in a

failure of justice the Court shall have regard to the fact whether the objections could and should have been raised at any earlier stage in the proceedings.

Explanation: For the purposes of this section.-

(a) error includes competency of the authority to grant sanction;

(b) a sanction required for prosecution includes reference to any requirement that the prosecution shall be at the instance of a specified authority or with the sanction of a specified person or any requirement of a similar nature.

20. Presumption where public servant accepts gratification other than legal remuneration.

(1) Where, in any trial of an offence punishable under Section 7 or Section 11 or clause (a) or clause (b) of sub-section (1) of Section-13 it is proved that an accused person has accepted or obtained or has agreed to accept or attempted to obtain for himself, or for any other person, any gratification (other than legal remuneration) or any valuable thing from any person, it shall be presumed, unless the contrary is proved, that he accepted or obtained or agreed to accept or attempted to obtain that gratification or that valuable thing, as the case may be, as a motive or reward such as is mentioned in section 7 or, as the case may be, without consideration or for a consideration which he knows to be inadequate.

(2) Where in any trial of an offence punishable under Section 12 or under clause (b) of Section –14, it is proved that any gratification (other than legal remuneration) or any valuable thing has been given or offered to be given or attempted to be given by an accused person, it shall be presumed, unless the contrary is proved, that he gave or offered to give or attempted to give

that gratification or that valuable thing, as the case may be, as a motive or reward such as is mentioned in section 7, or, as the case may be, without consideration or for a consideration which he knows to be inadequate.

(3) Notwithstanding anything contained in sub-sections (1) and (2), the Court may declined to draw the presumption referred to in either of the said sub-section, if the gratification or thing aforesaid is, in its opinion so trivial that no inference of corruption may fairly be drawn.

21. Accused person to be a competent witness. Any person charged with an offence punishable under this Act, shall be a competent witness for the defence and may give evidence on oath in disproof of the charges made against him or any person charged together with him at the same trial:

Provided that-

(a) he shall not be called as a witness except at his own request;

(b) his failure to give evidence shall not be made the subject of any comment by the prosecution or give rise to any presumption against himself or any person charged together with him at the same trial;

(c) he shall not be asked, and if asked shall not be required to answer, any question tending to show that he has committed or been convicted of any offence other than the offence with which he is charged, or if of bad character, unless.—

(i) the proof that he has committed or been convicted of such offence is admissible evidence to show that he is guilty of the offence with which he is charged, or

(ii) he has personally or by his pleader asked any question of any witness for the prosecution with a view to establish his own good character, or has given evidence of his good character, or the nature or conduct of the defence is such as to involve imputations on the character of the prosecutor or of any witness for the prosecution, or

(iii) he has given evidence against any other person charged with the same offence.

22. The Code of Criminal Procedure, 1973 to apply subject to certain modifications. The provisions of the Code of Criminal Procedure, 1973 (2 of 1974) shall in their application to any proceeding in relation to an offence punishable under this Act have effect as if.—

(a) in sub-section (1) Section 243, for the words "The accused shall then be called upon", the words "The accused shall then be required to give in writing at once or within such time as the Court may allow, a list of persons(if any) whom he proposes to examine as his witnesses and of the documents (if any) on which he proposes to rely and he shall then be called upon" had been substituted;

(b) in sub-section (2)of Section 309, after the third proviso the following proviso had been inserted, namely:-

"Provided also that the proceeding shall not be adjourned or postponed merely on the ground that an application under Section 397 has been made by a party to the proceeding."

(c) after sub-section (2) of Section 317, the following sub-section had been inserted, namely.-

"(3) Notwithstanding anything contained in sub-section (1) or sub-section (2), the Judge may if he thinks fit and for reasons to be recorded by him, proceed with inquiry or trial in the absence of the accused or his pleader and record the evidence of any witness subject to the right of the accused to recall the witness for cross-examination."

(d) in sub-section (1) of Section 397, before the Explanation, the following proviso had been inserted, namely.—

"Provided that where the powers under this section are exercised by a Court on an application made by a party to such proceedings, the Court shall not ordinarily call for the record of the proceedings."

(a) without giving the other party an opportunity of showing cause why the record should not be called for; or

(b) if it is satisfied that an examination of the record of the proceedings may be made from the certified copies."

23. Particulars in a charge in relation to an offence under Section 13(1)(c). Notwithstanding anything contained in the Code of Criminal Procedure, 1973(2 of 1974), when an accused is charged with an offence under clause (c) of sub-section (1) of Section 13, it shall be sufficient to describe in the charge the property in respect of which the offence is alleged to have been committed and the dates between which the offence is alleged to have been committed, without specifying particular items or exact dates, and the charge so framed shall be deemed to be a charge of one offence within the meaning of Section 219 of the said Code:

Provided that the time included between the first and last of such dates shall not exceed one year.

24.Statement by bribe giver not to subject him to prosecution. Notwithstanding anything contained in any law for the time being in force, a statement made by a person in any proceeding against a public servant for an offence under Sections 7 to 11 under Section 13 or Section 15, that he offered or agreed to offer any gratification(other than legal remuneration) or any valuable thing to the public servant, shall not subject such person to a prosecution under Section 12.

25. Military, Naval and Air Force or other law not to be affected.

(1) Nothing in this Act shall affect the jurisdiction exercisable by, or the procedure applicable, to, any Court or other authority under the Army Act, 1950(45 of 1950) the Air Force Act, 1950 (46 of 1950), the Navy Act, 1957 (62 of 1957), the Border Security Force Act, 1968 (47 of 1968), the Coast Guard Act, 1978 (30 of 1978), and the National Security Guard Act, 1986 (47 of 1986).

(2) For the removal of doubts, it is hereby declared that for the purposes of any such law as is referred to in sub-section (1), the Court of a Special Judge shall be deemed to be a Court of ordinary criminal justice.

26. Special Judges appointed under Act 46 of 1952 to be Special Judges appointed under this Act. Every Special Judge appointed under the Criminal Law Amendment Act, 1952, for any area or areas and is holding office on the commencement of this Act shall be deemed to be a Special Judge appointed under Section 3 of this Act for that area or areas and, accordingly, on and from such commencement, every such Judge shall continue to deal with all the proceedings pending before him on such commencement in accordance with the provisions if this Act.

27. Appeal and revision. Subject to the provisions of this Act, the High Court may exercise, so far as they may be applicable, all the powers of appeal and revision conferred by the Code of Criminal Procedure, 1973 (2 of 1974) on a High Court as if the Court of the Special Judge were a Court of Session trying cases within the local limits of the High Court.

28. Act to be in addition to any other law. The provisions of this Act shall be in addition to, and not in derogation of any other law for the time being in force, and nothing contained herein shall exempt any public servant from any proceeding which might, apart from this Act, be instituted against him.

29. Amendment of the Ordinance 38 of 1944. In the Criminal Law Amendment Ordinance, 1944—

(a) in sub-section (1) of Section 3, sub-section (1) of Section 9, clause (a) of Section 10, sub-section (1) of Section 11 and sub-section (1) of Section 13, for the words "State Government", wherever they occur, the words "State Government or, as the case may be, the Central Government" shall be substituted;

(b) in Section 10, in clause (a), for the words "three months", the words " one year " shall be substituted;

(c) in the Schedule.—

(i) paragraph 1 shall be omitted;

(ii) in paragraphs 2 and 4,—

(a) after the words " a local authority", the words and figures "or a corporation established by or under a Central Provincial or State Act, or an authority or a body owned or controlled or aided by Government or a Government Company as defined in Section 617 of the Companies Act, 1956 (1 of 1956), or a society aided by such corporation, authority, body or Government company" shall be inserted;

(b) after the words "or authority", the words "or corporation or body or Government company or society" shall be inserted;

(iii) for paragraph 4-A, the following paragraph shall be substituted, namely.—

"4-A. An offence punishable under the Prevention of Corruption Act, 1988."

(iv) in paragraph 5, for the words and figures "items 2,3 and 4", the words, figures and letter "items 2,3,4 and 4-A" shall be substituted.

30. Repeal and saving.

(1) The Prevention of Corruption Act, 1947, (2 of 1947) and the Criminal Law Amendment Act, 1952 (46 of 1952) are hereby repealed.

(2) Notwithstanding such repeal, but without prejudice to the application of Section 6 of the General Clauses Act, 1897 (10 of 1897), anything done or any action taken or purported to have been done or taken under or in pursuance of the Acts so repealed shall, in so far as it is not inconsistent with the provisions of this Act, be deemed to have been done or taken under or in pursuance of the corresponding provision of this Act.

31. Omission of certain sections of Act 45 of 1860. Sections 161 to 165-A (both inclusive) of the Indian Penal Code shall be omitted, and Section 6 of the General Clauses Act, 1897 (10 of 1897), shall apply to such omission as if the said sections had been repealed by a Central Act.

6

Anti-Corruption Movement 2011

Introduction

The 2011 Indian anti-corruption movement refers to a series of protests against the Government of India intended to seek strong legislation against graft, otherwise known as corruption. The protests have centred on a proposed bill, called the Jan Lokpal Bill, which the protestors believe could address the issue if it was suitably worded and enforced. The movement has gained momentum in particular since 5 April 2011, when Anna Hazare, a prominent activist, first went on a hunger strike which he called a "fast unto death".

The protesters are of the opinion that the government desires to dilute proposals contained in the original draft of the Jan Lokpal bill. They believe that the changes would make the body intended to oversee the issue, the Lokpal, no more than a powerless advisory body in the Indian bureaucracy. Hazare, who is a Gandhian, went on his initial hunger strike when talks designed to consider the issues broke down. He had demanded the creation of a joint drafting committee for the bill, with members from both "civil society" and government.

Following Hazare's initial, much publicised protest action, a second major protest saw controversial events take place at the Ramlila Maidan, New Delhi on 4 June 2011. The figurehead for these protests was Swami Ramdev and their aim was to highlight the need for strong legislation to bring back to the country what has been called "black money" deposited abroad. Ramdev demanded that untaxed money invested abroad should be declared to be the wealth of the nation and, further, that the act of caching money alleged to have been obtained illegally in foreign banks should be declared a crime against the state. He also demanded that the nation's wealth held in foreign banks should be brought back and that India should sign the United Nations Convention against Corruption. It is estimated that around US$ 350 billion to US$ 1400 billion worth of illegal money is in foreign banks.

The protests led to the creation of a movement that saw protests being organised in various cities and towns of India. Protests included fasts, candlelight vigils and rallies. The protests are unusual in India as they have no political affiliation and the protesters have been hostile to any attempt by political parties to use them to strengthen their own political agenda.

Background

The 2011 Indian anti-corruption movement refers to a series of protests against the Government of India intended to seek strong legislation against graft, otherwise known as corruption. The protests have centred on a proposed bill, called the Jan Lokpal Bill, which the protestors believe could address the issue if it was suitably worded and enforced. The movement has gained momentum in particular since 5 April 2011, when Anna Hazare, a prominent activist, first went on a hunger strike which he called a "fast unto death".

Issues regarding corruption in India have become more prominent in recent years. The country was subject to socialist-inspired economic policies between the 1950s and the late 1980s. Extensive regulation, protectionism, and public ownership led to slow growth. The system of bureaucratic controls called License Raj was at the core of corruption.

The Vohra Report of 1993, submitted by the former Indian Union Home Secretary N. N. Vohra, studied the problem of the criminalization of politics and of the nexus among criminals, politicians and bureaucrats in India. The report contained several observations made by official agencies on the criminal network which was virtually running a parallel government. It also discussed criminal gangs who enjoyed the patronage of politicians of all political parties and the protection of government functionaries. It revealed that political leaders had become the leaders of gangs. They were also connected to the military. Over the years criminals had been elected to local bodies, State Assemblies, and even the Parliament.

The Right to Information Act of 2005 has helped civilians work effectively towards tackling corruption. It allows Indian citizens (except those living in Jammu and Kashmir) to request information, for a fixed fee of 10 (US$ 0.22), from a "public authority" (a body of Government or "instrumentality of State") which is required to reply expeditiously or within thirty days. Activists have used this to uncover graft cases against various politicians and bureaucrats, one consequence being that some of those activists have been attacked and even killed.

Various scandals were discovered in 2010-2011, including the 2G spectrum scam, Adarsh Housing Society Scam, and the Commonwealth Games scam. These involved various Ministers and also members of the Armed Forces, and they demonstrated how entrenched corruption had become in India. They led also to popular, non-political movements campaigning to fight graft via new legislation.

The Jan Lokpal Bill, also referred to as the Citizens' Ombudsman Bill, is a proposal to establish an independent body to investigate cases of corruption within a year and to ensure a speedy prosecution within two years of an investigation being started. The Jan Lokpal Bill was proposed by members of the civil society (primarily social activists from the NGO India Against Corruption as an alternative to the Government-drafted Lokpal Bill. The August 16 protests started as a result of significant disagreements over the two versions of the Bill between the civil society leaders and the Government.

Protest Timeline

A poster against corruption in India

- A group of Delhi residents drove around the city dressed in similar clothing in an attempt to raise awareness of corruption issues and to gain support for the Jan Lokpal Bill.

28 March 2011 (2011-03-28)

- There were protest marches in various cities across the world, including some in the US. These included a 240-mile march in California that began on 12 March in San Diego and ended on 26 March at the statue erected in honour of Gandhi in San Francisco.

30 March 2011 (2011-03-30)

- Kapil Dev, a former captain of the Indian national cricket team, wrote a letter to the Prime Minister, Manmohan Singh, complaining that the many investigations into scams arising from the recent Commonwealth Games had achieved nothing so far. He said that, "Why can't we have an independent Lokpal to look into these scams? I consider you as the cleanest politician in the recent history and I urge you for a Jan Lokpal Bill".

4 April 2011 (2011-04-04)

- Hazare announced that he would commence his "fast unto death" and that this would last until a comprehensive measure to tackle corruption was introduced. He claimed that the government had excluded "civil society" from the panel set up to draft the Jan Lokpal Bill, and implied that at least one of the people who was to be on the drafting committee - Sharad Pawar - might be unsuitable for that role because of his large landholdings. Kiran Bedi and Swami Agnivesh voiced their support for Hazare.

5 April 2011 (2011-04-05)

Protesters have come out in support of Anna Hazare

- Hazare initiated his fast at Jantar Mantar in Delhi. Elsewhere, people attended a protest at Freedom Park, Bangalore.
- Campaigners for India Against Corruption (IAC) estimated that a petition circulated in the city of Pune which demanded that the government enact a bill had attracted between 5000 and 6000 signatures between 3 April and 5 April. Hazare has been involved with IAC, a group established by various prominent activists with the primary purpose of achieving the legal enactment and subsequent enforcement of a strong version of the Jan Lokpal bill.

7 April 2011 (2011-04-07)

Protests have continued as the Government fails to offer better terms to the activists

- Two rounds of talks failed. There was agreement regarding constituting a panel to examine the Bill but the government would not accede to demands that it should be a formally constituted panel or that Hazare should lead it. As a consequence of this, Hazare continued his fast.
- Narendra Modi, the Chief Minister of Gujarat lashes out at Manmohan Singh for resisting the passage of the Jan Lokpal Bill.
- Sonia Gandhi, the president of the Indian National Congress party and the head of the National Advisory Council appealed to Hazare to end his indefinite fast.
- Hazare and the protesters tried to keep the protests

non-political. No politicians were welcome at the site of the fast. Former Haryana Chief Minister Om Prakash Chautala, former Madhya Pradesh Chief Minister Uma Bharti and journalist Barkha Dutt were forced by civilians to leave, after the protesters objected to their presence, which they believed was harming the integrity of their movement.

8 April 2011 (2011-04-08)

Protesters in Pune

- Protests spread to numerous other places, including Mumbai, Kolkata, Thiruvananthapuram, Hyderabad, Jaipur, Chennai, Patna, Bhopal, Ahmedabad, Ranchi, Pune, and the University of Jammu.
- The government continued to squabble with the activists stating that the bill drafting committee will be headed by a government appointed minister and not a civil society member as the protesters demanded to avoid allowing the government to make the bill less powerful.
- The Prime Minister, Manmohan Singh, met with the President of India to outline to her how the government was going ahead with the demands of the population.
- 15 supporters of Hazare on fast were hospitalized.
- Bollywood came out in support of the protests, with actors, musicians and directors speaking in support of the movement and Hazare. Director Farah Khan, actor Anupam Kher, music director Vishal Dadlani, poet-filmmaker Pritish Nandy and actor Tom Alter all visited Jantar Mantar; others stated their support for the movement via social networking websites or the media. Oscar winning Indian composer A. R. Rahman also declared his support for the anti-graft movement.
- Renowned Indian/Qatari artist Late M. F. Hussain showed his support by drawing a cartoon of Hazare.
- Indian students at Cambridge University, the former

alma mater of the Indian Prime Minister also expressed their support for the movement.

- Many prominent people from government agencies as well as from various corporate houses came out in support of the movement. Some of them were - Delhi Metro chief E. Sreedharan. (also called the Metro Man of India), Punj Lloyd chairman Atul Punj, Maruti Suzuki chairman R. C. Bhargava, Hero group's Sunil Munjal, Tata Steel vice-chairman B Muthuraman, Bajaj Auto Chairman Rahul Bajaj, Godrej Group head Adi Godrej, Biocon Chairman and Managing Director Kiran Mazumdar-Shaw and Kotak Mahindra Bank vice-chairman & managing director Uday Kotak. They all declared their support for Hazare and the movement.
- ASSOCHAM President Dilip Modi and FICCI Director General Rajiv Kumar, too came out in support of the movement.
- The Government of India accepted the compromise formula that there be a politician chairman and an activist non-politician Co-Chairman. It was reported that Pranab Mukherjee will be the Chairman of the draft committee while Shanti Bhushan will be the co-chairman. Bhushan was one of the original drafters of the Lokpal Bill along with Hazare, Justice N. Santosh Hegde, advocate Prashant Bhushan, and RTI activist Arvind Kejriwal.

9 April 2011 (2011-04-09)

- After accepting all the demands of Hazare, the Government of India issued a Official Gazette saying that the draft of the lokpal would be made and presented in the coming monsoon session of Lok Sabha.
- Victory celebrations took place at locations throughout the country and even Hazare's village.
- Bollywood lauded the outcome, repeating their support for the movement.

- Protesters and leaders of the movement alike stated that the path to attaining complete passage of the bill is still a difficult one, and the movement may see harsher days ahead.
- Many commentators have called the movement the 'wake-up' call for India.
- Within a day of the beginning of the agitation, more than 30,000 people had pledged their support to the Lokpal Bill. Organisers of the India Against Corruption said 30,000 people from Maharashtra expressed their support on their website. The website has 20,000 members in Mumbai alone. Within a few days the Facebook page for India Against Corruption had more than 220,000 likes.

16 April 2011 (2011-04-16)

- The first meeting regarding a draft of the Lokpal Bill was held on 16 April. The government agreed to audio-record all meetings of the Lokpal Bill panel and to hold public consultations before a final draft is prepared. Hazare demanded that the proceedings be televised live but the government refused.

4 June 2011 (2011-06-04)

- Swami Ramdev begins his indefinite hunger strike at Ramlila Maidan in Delhi to bring back the black money stashed in tax havens abroad.
- 65,000 followers gathered at Ramlila Maidan.
- In a press conference in the evening Kapil Sibbal made public a letter from Ramdev's camp to call off the hunger strike. Ramdev took it as a betrayal and hardened his position.

5 June 2011 (2011-06-05)

- At midnight, police raided the grounds when most protesters were sleeping and Ramdev was busy at a meeting with his core group.

- A large police force lobbed tear gas shells, burned the place and lathicharge the crowd at 1 am (IST) to evict them.
- Police had arranged buses to drop supporters at railway stations and bus stands in advance; had ammunition ready and were in battle-gear wearing vests and helmets and kept some ambulances on standby.
- Delhi Police arrested Ramdev, who was disguised in a salwar kameez with a group of female protesters heading peacefully towards the New Delhi Railway Station
- Ramdev was held in a government guesthouse for a few hours and then sent to Dehradun in a BSF aircraft.
- Ramdev was sent to his Patanjali Yogpeeth ashram in Haridwar where he delivered a press conference.
- 53 people were injured and were treated at the Lok Nayak Jai Prakash (LNJP) hospital, AIIMS Trauma Center and Ram Manohar Lohia Hospital.
- One of Baba Ramdev's supporters was injured in the incident and her condition was still critical as on 17th August 2011.
- Protesters huddled near the Metro station, bus depots and railway stations. Many walked down to Gurdwara Bangla Sahib and other nearby ashrams. According to New Delhi railway station authorities, supporters continued to leave in batches through the course of the day. While several supporters spent the day at a park near Ramlila Maidan, others took shelter at an Arya Samaj facility in Paharganj.
- Ramdev was prohibited from entering Delhi for 15 days.

6 June 2011 (2011-06-06)

- Prime Minister Manmohan Singh justified the action against Baba Ramdev as an operation that had to be conducted, and that there was no alternative. However Manmohan Singh did not elaborate as to why force was used on a peaceful gathering and why the swoop was done at 1 AM in the morning.

9 June 2011 (2011-06-09)

- Hazare described his fight against corruption as the "Second Freedom Struggle" and set an ultimatum of 15 August 2011, as the last date to pass a strong Jan Lokpal Bill, threatening to otherwise intensify his anti-corruption agitation and start another fast from 16 August.

16 June 2011 (2011-06-16)

- The Government and the civil society split wide open due to differences in jointly drafting the bill. Government representatives said that if a consensus on the common bill was not reached, two drafts would be sent to the Cabinet, one drafted by the Government and the other drafted by the civil society. Team Anna also claimed that only 15 points, out of a total 71 recommended, were agreed upon and included in the joint draft. Hazare declared that if the government version of the bill was passed in the Parliament, he would start his hunger strike from August 16, 2011.

22 June 2011 (2011-06-22)

- In a veiled warning to Anna Hazare for his proposed fast, Congress leader Digvijay Singh on Wednesday indicated that the Gandhian might be meted out the same treatment, depending upon the prevailing situation at that time, as yoga guru Ramdev was given at Ramlila ground.

14 August 2011 (2011-08-14)

- In a scathing attack on Anna Hazare, Congress spokesperson, Manish Tewari, and an MP from Ludhiana constituency, described Anna Hazare as being "involved in corruption from top to bottom", "neck deep in corruption", and also mentioning that the social activist needed to be "shown his place".

15 August 2011 (2011-08-15)

- Anna Hazare announced at a press conference that he and his supporters were determined to go ahead with the fast on 16 August, 2011 as planned. He also urged people to court arrest to push for a stronger Lokpal bill.
- Section 144 was imposed a night before the planned protest date, at JP Park, Rajghat and Dilli Gate, which prohibited assembly of five or more persons.

16 August 2011 (2011-08-16)

- Anna Hazare was detained by Delhi Police in the early morning before he could start his hunger strike at JP park, Delhi. Delhi Police had asked Anna not to leave his home, which he declined, and Anna was detained at his residence in Mayur Vihar. Arvind Kejriwal, Kiran Bedi, Manish Sisodia and more than 1200 supporters were also taken into preventive custody by the Police.
- Anna Hazare was sent to seven days judicial custody to Tihar jail after refusing to sign a personal bond to be released on bail.
- Shehla Masood, an RTI activist and a strong supporter of Anna Hazare's anti-corruption movement, was shot dead around 11.30am IST. An unidentified assailant shot her in front of her house in Koh-e-Fiza, Bhopal.
- Kiran Bedi and Shanti Bhushan, detained by Delhi Police on the morning ahead of Anna Hazare's fast-unto-death, were released in the evening at around 6:30pm IST.
- The current telecom minister Kapil Sibal was greeted with black flags and booed by a group of students at a seminar on the Jan Lokpal bill.
- With the Government of India, preparing to release Anna Hazare late in the night, however Anna refused to come out of Tihar jail until the government agreed

to an unconditional permission to hold protests at JP Park.

- Demonstrations were held all over India protesting Anna Hazare's arrest. In Chennai, Mahatma Gandhi's secretary, V Kalyanam led the protestors. He said - "India will get a sure gold medal if corruption is entered as an item in the Olympic Games. We may not be a force in football or athletics or hockey. But India is the undisputed global leader in corruption." Referring to Anna Hazare's arrest in New Delhi, Kalyanam said it was easier to fight foreign tyranny than the tyranny of our own people. He ridiculed the contention of Union ministers like Kapil Sibal and Chidambaram that Parliament was supreme and civil society had no voice.

17 August 2011 (2011-08-17)

- After almost a day, Anna still refused to leave jail and spent the night in a room in Tihar jail, despite the government decision to free him.
- Delhi Police made concessions for Anna Hazare to fast, stepping up from seven days to 14 days and finally 21 days at Ramlila Maidan.
- Congress made a statement that they suspected a foreign hand in the protests and asked the government to probe if the US was behind Anna's agitation .

18 August 2011 (2011-08-18)

- Anna Hazare agreed to leave jail after Delhi Police granted him permission to fast for 15-days against corruption at Ramlila Maidan. However, he would spend another night in Jail till the venue is ready.
- Arvind Kejriwal left Tihar jail being there for two days. Kejriwal called this move as just the beginning of their fight against corruption, and also confirmed that Anna Hazare would leave the jail once the grounds at Ramlila Maidan are ready for the fast.

19 August 2011 (2011-08-19)

- Anna Hazare left Tihar Jail at 15 minutes to noon IST after 3 days with spontaneous roar of welcome from the huge crowd accumulated near the Jail premises. Just passed the gates, he raised his hand in the air and shouted "Bharat mata ki Jai (Victory to Mother India)". He also addressed public stating: "Whether I am there or not, this fight will continue." which too recieved a huge roar of applause. Anna waved national flag towards the crowd, responsing the crowd fluttered hundreds of smaller flags and chanted "Anna zindabad (long live Anna)".
- Paying obeisance to Mahatma Gandhi at Rajghat and Amar Jawan Jyoti at the India Gate, Anna Hazare reached Delhi's Ramlila Maidan to launch 15-day mass protest against corruption.
- Anna Hazare finally launched his protest at Ramlila Maidan as he declared that he will not quit the venue till the Jan Lokpal Bill is brought.
- Varun Gandhi, Bharatiya Janata Party MP announced that he will introduce Anna Hazare's Jan Lokpal Bill in the Lok Sabha as a private member's bill by saying that Jan Lokpal Bill is better than anything the nation has seen before and would like to make a small contribution in his own way.

21 August 2011 (2011-08-21)

- Anna Hazare's camp on Sunday called their supporters to confront individual Members of Parliament and Union Ministers at their residence and also warned the UPA government that its days would be numbered if it failed to pass the Bill by August 30.
- Over 100,000 supporters had thronged Ramlila Maidan on Sunday, to show their support against corruption.
- Around 50,000 supporters marched in the streets on Mumbai to support Anna Hazare's call for an effective anti-corruption legislation. The marchers started from

the Bandra railway station and walked all the way to Juhu, reportedly in one of the biggest protests in Mumbai.

Government Response

Hazare's protest has led to the resignation of Agriculture Minister Sharad Pawar from the Group of Ministers on corruption. On 8 April, the government started seriously considering the demands of the protesters. The government has stated that it will table the bill in the parliament in the upcoming Monsoon session. On 9 April, the government finally agreed to have a 50:50 distribution of the Government appointed officials and the members of the civil society. On May 13, PM Manmohan Singh stated that the Indian government has completed the process for ratification of UN Convention against Corruption.

Political Response at the Jantar Mantar Protests

Bhartiya Janata Party: The Bhartiya Janata Party supported Hazare, with a prominent member, Arun Jaitley, urging the government to take Hazare's fast very seriously.

Another prominent BJP figure, L.K. Advani suggested that a meeting of political parties should be convened to discuss the issue "particularly in the context of black money and curbing money-power in elections".

BJP leader Narendra Modi posted on his Facebook account that he was praying for Hazare's health. He also published an open letter to Hazare thanking him for the latter's support for the development work in Gujarat. Modi also warned Hazare of possible vilification by a certain 'powerful-group' that wishes to defame Modi and Gujarat. He reiterated his support for the Jan Lokpal Bill.

Communist Party of India (Marxist): The Communist Party of India (Marxist) came out in support of Anna Hazare.

Prakash Karat pledged support to Hazare over the Jan Lokpal Bill.

Ramlila Ground Protests

Ramdev claimed that Bharat Swabhiman Yatra had evoked massive support from the masses and more than 10 crore people had been directly involved with the movement. His yatra ended on June 1 at Ujjain in Madhya Pradesh after traveling over 100,000 kilometres (62,000 mi) across the country. Almost 3.2 million "netizens" joined the campaign.

Ramdev declared that a people's movement to liberate the country from rampant corruption and build a strong spiritual 'Bharat' would be launched by him in June. The movement was called "Satyagraha against Corruption". He declared one of the main objectives of the movement was to bring about an end to corruption and bring back black money stashed away in various financial institutions in the country and abroad. On the midnight of 5 June, police raided the site where Ramdev was fasting against corruption and black money issues in the capital and forcefully detained him and removed his supporters from the site after firing tear gas shells and resorting to lathicharge to end his day-old indefinite hunger strike on black money issue. Seventy-one people were injured and moved to hospital, four of whom were reported to be in critical condition. Finance Minister Pranab Mukherjee called the police action "unfortunate", but added that the government had to do that as Ramdev had no permission to hold a protest at the Ramlila Ground.

He maintained that second phase of Bharat Swabhiman Yatra would begin from October 2011 year and the Yatra would once again travel a distance of 100,000 kilometres (62,000 mi).

Background to the Ramlila ground protests: On March 16, 2011, the Communist Party of India (Marxist) issued its manifesto for the upcoming Bengal polls in 2011, which said that "if the party came to power, it would launch a drive to unearth black money, especially those stashed in Swiss and other tax havens." The issue was taken up by Sharad Yadav of Janata Dal (United), who said on March 27 that there were US$ 1,470 billion stashed by Indians in Swiss banks.

Four senior Union Ministers Pranab Mukherjee, Kapil Sibal, Pawan Kumar Bansal and Subodh Kant Sahay met Ramdev and discussed issues and his demands at Delhi Airport on June 1, 2011. Back-channel talk between two sides were held in The Claridges, New Delhi on June 2, 2011. Next day talks were held for a third time between the ministers and Ramdev and both sides claimed consensus. The government gave a response to the demands while Ramdev planned to go ahead with his hunger strike.

250,000 square metres (2,700,000 sq ft) of overhead waterproof tent was set up and the ground was booked for 40 days for the protest. A volunteer centre at the extreme end of the maidan was set up. 650 bathrooms and toilets was stationed inside the maidan, out of which 40 percent were for women. Also provided for was drinking water facility, medical facility and a media centre with three communication towers.

Police action against the Demonstration

Police fired tear gas, burned the place and lathicharged peacefully fasting men, women and children. 53 persons were reportedly injured and were treated at the Lok Nayak Jai Prakash (LNJP) hospital, AIIMS trauma center and Ram Manohar Lohia Hospital.

About 5000 supporters were still missing according to Ramdev. Jadeep Arya, a key advisor on Ramdev's team, said that about 19 girls students from the Chotipur Gurukul who were seated near the dais were thought to be still missing. Behen Suman, women's representative of the Trust, said many of these girls were roughed up when the police tried to reach Ramdev and were crying since police officials were pulling their hair, dragging them and their clothes were torn. Police, however, said no one was missing.

There is an allegation that CCTV footage of the raid is missing.

Police Clarification on Action

A senior police officer commented on the police action saying, "there were talks in the police headquarters since June 2 that Baba Ramdev would be detained as we knew he is definitely not going to hold a Yoga camp." Allegedly, Ramdev's detention was not a spontaneous decision but had been planned for several days.

The police said Ramdev was informed around 11 pm (IST) on Saturday that his permission to continue his agitation had been canceled. By that time, over 5000 police officers, including 12 battalions of the Delhi Police, three battalions of Rapid Action Force, two of Central Reserve Police Force commandos and local police were briefed by senior police officers to get ready for action. The Ramlila Ground was then surrounded by several buses and tempos, heading towards the ground from Haryana, Rajasthan, Uttar Pradesh and Punjab but were sent back from the borders.

Protest against Police Action on Ramdev's Demonstration

On 6 June the National Human Rights Commission of India issued notices to the Union Home Secretary, Delhi Chief Secretary and the Delhi City Commissioner of Police seeking reports within two weeks regarding the midnight crackdown at the Ramlila Ground.

In a response to the crackdown Hazare said that he would hold a one day hunger strike at Jantar Mantar on 8 June. The venue was changed to Rajghat when he could not get police permission to do so.

Aftermath of the Ramlila Ground Protests

Protests were held in many different parts of country, including the cities of Bangalore, Mumbai, Hyderabad, Jammu, and Lucknow. Protests against the action also spread to Nepal.

Civil Society Response

Ramdev accused the government of not being serious about discussing issues of corruption and black money, alleging that government negotiator Kapil Sibal had cheated him through "scheming and cunning" attitude. He alleged that there was a conspiracy to kill him and a "threat" was given to him during a meeting with senior ministers. He also claimed that the ruling government chairperson Sonia Gandhi and the United Progressive Alliance government will be responsible for any threat to his life and alleged that he was nearly strangled by the police. After being evicted from Delhi, Ramdev wanted to continue his fast from Noida but was denied permission to do so by the Uttar Pradesh government. He decided to continue his hunger strike and satyagraha from Haridwar only until June 12, 2011.

Hazare said there might have been some faults with Ramdev's agitation but that the beating up of people at night rather than in the day-time was a "blot on democracy" and that "There was no firing otherwise the eviction was similar to Jallianwala Bagh incident." He said that the "strangulation of democracy" would cause civil society to launch protests throughout the country to "teach government a lesson". Other civil society leaders, such as Arvind Kejriwal, also termed the use of police force on non-violent sleeping protesters as undemocratic. Shanti Bhushan and Swami Agnivesh also criticised the police action to end the hunger strike.

Government Response

Congress General Secretary Digvijay Singh called Ramdev a "cheat" and "fraud". According to him the government had reached an agreement before the protests were held. Prime Minister Manmohan Singh wrote to Ramdev, asking to cease-and-desist from holding the protests. Nationalist Congress Party General Secretary Tariq Anwar said that "Both Hazare and Ramdev are blackmailing the government and they should first peep into their own hearts." Pawan Bansal commented on the midnight police action and said that "It was not a crackdown, we the government had to do it to maintain law and order".

Other Political Parties Response

- **Bharatiya Janata Party:** The party called the police action to break up the hunger strike "undemocratic". BJP President Nitin Gadkari said they will organize a 24-hour long Satyagraha at Rajghat independent of government's permission. Nitin Gadkari further added; "Women and children were attacked. They were lathi charged and teargas was used. This reminds us of the Emergency days in 1975. We strongly condemn it," and "The Prime Minister and Sonia Gandhi used force on democratic ways of protest against corruption and black money. I condemn the action of Manmohan Singh and Sonia Gandhi. They should apologize for the act," Gujarat Chief Minister Narendra Modi strongly condemned the incident comparing atrocities on Ramlila ground by comparing the government with Ravana-Lila further adding that "It is one of the worst days of Indian history. The Prime Minister had said during the elections that he would bring back black money stashed in Swiss banks within 100 days of coming into power. But today, it is two years and nothing has happened." Senior BJP leader Lal Krishna Advani said that the police action reminded him of the Jallianwala Bagh massacre and added that the police crackdown on Ramdev is a "naked fascism". Leader of the Opposition in the Lok Sabha Sushma Swaraj said: "This is not democracy the police cannot alone had taken such a step. It had the approval of the Prime Minister and full approval of the Congress President.

- **Bahujan Samaj Party:** BSP leader and Uttar Pradesh Chief Minister, Mayawati, condemned the government's midnight crackdown on Ramdev and demanded that Supreme Court of India order an investigation into the incident stating that justice cannot be expected from the Central Government.
- **Samajwadi Party:** Samajwadi Party chief Mulayam Singh Yadav condemned the incident saying that the action shows Centre has lost its mental balance. Charging the ruling Congress Party, Yadav further said: "A Congress leader said that Baba is a thug. I want to say that Congress is the biggest thug and it should introspect its deeds. "The government swooped down on Ramdev and his supporters as if it were carrying an attack on a foreign enemy," Yadav told reporters at a press conference.
- **Rashtriya Janata Dal:** RJD leader Lalu Prasad Yadav accused Ramdev of being a front for the Rashtriya Swayamsevak Sangh.
- **Communist Party of India (Marxist):** CPI(M) termed the police action at the protest site of Ramdev as "deplorable and shortsighted". However, they found fault with the yoga guru for making the issue of black money "farcical" by entering into a secret agreement with government. "The manner in which Ramdev's demands were drafted and the way in which he has conducted his interactions with the government,

coming to a secret agreement to withdraw the hunger strike on the basis of assurances, then reneging and announcing its extension trivialised the seriousness of the issue of black money and made it farcical," the party said.

- **Shiv Sena:** The Shiv Sena strongly condemned the police action against Ramdev.
- Janata Dal (United): Nitish Kumar, leader of JD(U) and the Chief Minister of Bihar, condemned the attack saying "It is a major blow to democracy and an attack on the democractic rights of the people. It is also an attack on the fundamental rights of the citizens."

Suo Moto Cognizance by the Supreme Court

The Supreme Court of India issued notices to the Union Home Secretary, Chief Secretary of Delhi, Delhi administration, and Delhi Police Commissioner asking them to respond within two weeks, after taking suo motu cognizance of forceful eviction of Ramdev and his followers from the Ramlila ground.

However, the court declined to entertain a petition filed by advocate Ajay Aggarwal, who said that no FIR had been registered against the police officials. The bench expressed its displeasure that before the matter came up for hearing before it, the entire contents of the petition were leaked to the media.

August Protests

Background: On July 18, 2011, Hazare declared that he had written a letter to the Prime Minister about his decision to go on an indefinite fast from August 16 at Jantar Mantar. Hazare said that it was the right of Indian citizens to protest and the government could not crush their movement, unlike the Ramlila ground protests. Hazare declared that he was ready to get arrested and beaten up and informed the Delhi Police about his protest.

Hazare's crusade for a strong Lokpal Bill found support in Mumbai as the Mumbai Taximen's Union, comprising over 30,000 taxis, agreed to extend their support to Hazare's cause on August 16. The union's decision came after a meeting with Hazare's team in Mumbai. The union's proposal was to keep all taxis off the roads or ply less taxis on August 16. The Mumbai chapter of India Against Corruption claimed that till July 26, nearly 44,000 people had shown interest in joining the protest from August 16.

In Allahabad, the legal community expressed their support of Hazare's campaign against corruption. Lawyers of Allahabad High Court held protests in support of Anna Hazare at Allahabad by burning copies of the Lokpal Bill, blocking roads and shouting slogans against the callousness of the government. They also pledged to go on a hunger strike at Allahabad from August 16 in support of Anna Hazare.

The Vishwa Hindu Parishad also came out in support of Hazare's movement, saying that for a strong Lokpal, people from across the country should support the campaign.

In a referendum conducted by India Against Corruption in Karnataka, about 94.3% of Chikkaballapur constituency and 79.7% of Bangalore South voted to bring the prime minister under the ambit of the Jan Lokpal Bill. The results showed that a majority of the population wanted the Jan Lokpal Bill to be passed by the Parliament and not the "watered down, toothless" bill drafted by the government. The 6,000 participants at the referendum also said that being representatives of the people, members of parliament should vote for the Lokpal, not as directed by their parties, but as by the voice of the majority in his/her constituency. The participants also voted to bring judges under the Lokpal, give adequate powers to the Lokpal to dismiss officers guilty of corruption, monitor corruption at the central as well as state level through Lokayuktas, and to bring all levels of officers under the bill. The questionnaire had a set of eight questions that brought out crucial differences between the Jan Lokpal

Bill and the Lokpal Bill put forth by the government, and asked for the people's vote on the same. Around ten parliamentary constituencies across the nation conducted a similar exercise and the results from the nation-wide campaign will be consolidated and presented to the members of Parliament in time for the monsoon session.

Hazare's Arrest

On the morning of August 16, 2011, Hazare, along with close associates, was remanded to judicial custody for seven days. Hazare was picked up by police at about 7.30am from a residence in east Delhi for "intending to defy prohibitory orders". Late afternoon, he was produced before a special executive magistrate. After he refused to sign a personal bond to be allowed to get out on bail he was remanded in judicial custody for seven days. Within hours of his detention, a spokesperson for Team Anna said that he had begun his hunger protest while in police custody and that he was not accepting even water to drink. The arrest of Hazare and some of his close associates, set off a groundswell of protests across the country and this appeared to be spreading quickly. The arrest was condemned by political parties, the chief ministers of some non-Congress ruled states, non-government organizations and even parliament did not transact any business after an uproar on the issue forced an adjournment for the day.

As protests built up in several cities and towns over the arrest, Prashant Bhushan, one of Hazare's key associates, announced a march from India Gate to Parliament House on Wednesday to protest against the police action, which he said was taken at the behest of some cabinet ministers. Delhi police commissioner BK Gupta said that the police were not keen for Hazare be sent to judicial custody. He said police were prepared to release him on a personal bond if he would have given an undertaking that he would not defy Section 144 of the Criminal Procedure Code which prohibits the gathering of five or more people and ask his supporters not to do so also. Hazare was taken to the Tihar jail where he will spend the time in judicial custody. Kiran Bedi, Arvind Kejriwal and Manoj Sisodia, three other leading activists of team Anna, have also been sent to judicial custody on similar grounds. In a message released after his detention, Hazare said this was the beginning of the "second freedom struggle" and he called on people to participate in a "jail bharo" agitation.

Opposition parties, peeved over the attitude of the Congress in Parliament, said they would meet later today to decide on the course of action. Communist Party of India leader Gurudas Dasgupta said he had proposed a boycott of parliament for three days. Communist Party of India (Marxist) leader Brinda Karat described the arrest as "a strong attack on democratic rights". Hours after arrest of Hazare, Leader of Opposition in Lok Sabha and BJP leader Sushma Swaraj strongly condemned the action and demanded and explanation from Prime Minister, Manmohan Singh saying that the government is hell-bent on crushing the civil rights of the citizens. Senior Bhartiya Janata Party leader L K Advani said he was not surprised at the detention of Mr Hazare and he charged the government with looking for scapegoats and stopping peaceful protests instead of fighting corruption. Arun Jaitley, leader of the opposition in the Rajya Sabha, said, that it was a very sad day for Indian democracy, where the ruling government took away the right to protest and the right to dissent.

In Patna, Bihar chief minister Nitish Kumar described the detention of Hazare and his associates as a "rehearsal of emergency" which people will never tolerate, and "a murder of democracy." Punjab chief minister Prakash Singh Badal also condemned the arrests saying that the Congress has panicked over the movement of Anna Hazare and accused Congress leaders of stashing money abroad. In Chandigarh and Ludhiana, people from all walks of life took to the streets despite inclement weather to join the protest for a strong Lokpal. Among them were activists of the NGOs 'India Against

Corruption' and 'Awaaz' who launched a relay hunger strike. Traffic was also blocked at several intersections. Slamming the Centre for detaining Anna Hazare and his aides, Bihar Deputy Chief Minister SK Modi today called upon the people to come to the streets to hold demonstration in support of Anna's movement against corruption "peacefully and democratically."

In Hyderabad, Telugu Desam Party president N. Chandrababu Naidu asked the Prime minister Manmohan Singh to apologize to the nation for having sent Hazare and other social activists, who are fighting against corruption, to Tihar jail. In Maharashtra, crowds gathered in many cities and towns in response to Mr Hazare's call to court arrest. Thousands poured into south Mumbai's Azad Maidan since early in the morning, in preparation for the 'Jail Bharo' programme. A large number of people courted arrest in support of the demand for an effective Lokpal. Many people wearing 'Gandhi' caps with slogans 'I am Anna' gathered at the Reserve Bank of India Square, on the busy Nagpur-Jabalpur national highway that runs through the Civil Lines area.

In a broad day light murder at Bhopal, capital of Madhya Pradesh, an RTI activist and a strong supporter of Anna Hazare's anti-corruption movement, Shehla Masood was shot dead around 11.30 am on August 16. An unidentified assailant shot her dead from point blank range while she was leaving in her car to attend a demonstration in support of Anna Hazare.

In Delhi, in protest against the arrest of Anna Hazare and his close aides by the Delhi Police, the members of All India Students Association showed black flags and shouted anti-government slogan against Kapil Sibal, who was to address a seminar at Malvankar Hall in city.

Anna on August 16 asked government employees across the country to go on mass leave to show solidarity with the movement. Union Home minister P. Chidambaram hoped they would not respond, describing the call as "completely wrong." Hazare's close associate and lawyer Prashant Bhushan urged government servants to join their cause and take a mass leave for a day and join the protests in their city.

Release

After protests all over India, the Delhi Police decided to release Hazare after he had been sent to Tihar Jail for seven days. Hazare had even refused food and water intake in Tihar jail, indicating he would carry on his fast in jail. Hazare and his aides, including Kiran Bedi and Arvind Kejriwal, were first taken to the Delhi Police Officer's Mess in North Delhi and were shifted to another after Hazare's supporters gathered in large numbers at Civil Lines. The Delhi Police sent a warrant to the Tihar Jail for the release of Hazare and his supporters withdrawing bail bond conditions, which Hazare had earlier refused to sign. Over 1,500 people who have been detained for taking part in protests demanding Hazare's release were released. Congress sources said that the Government decided to release Hazare and his supporters after coming to the conclusion that keeping him in jail would disrupt law and order unnecessarily. The decision to release Hazare was made after Prime Minister Manmohan Singh met party General Secretary Rahul Gandhi, who disapproved of the arrest, on the evening of August 16. Hazare supporters Kiran Bedi and Shanti Bhushan were released by the Delhi Police early on August 16. However, on release, Anna Hazare refused to leave Tihar jail until the government agreed to give unconditional permission to hold protests at JP Park.

Anna Hazare agreed to leave jail after Delhi Police granted him permission to fast for 15 days against corruption at Ramlila Maidan, a larger venue than JP Park. However, he had to spend another night in jail as the venue was not ready. On 19 August, at around 12 noon IST, Anna left Tihar jail after 3 days. Supporters welcomed him with spontaneous roar as he headed towards Delhi's Ramlila Maidan to launch his hunger protest.

7

Lokpal Bill by Government of India

The Lokpal Bill, 2010

A BILL to provide for the establishment of the institution of Lokpal to inquire into allegations of corruption against public functionaries and for matters connected therewith.

BE it enacted by parliament in the Sixty-first Year of the Republic of India as follows:-

CHAPTER - I : PRELIMINARY

1. Short title and commencement.

(1) This Act may be called the Lokpal Act, 2010.

(2) It shall come into force on such date as the central Government may, by notification in the official Gazette, appoint.

2. Definitions. In this Act, unless the context otherwise requires,-

(1) "Chairperson" means the Chairperson of the Lokpal;

(2) "Competent authority", in relation to–

(i) the Prime Minister, means the house of the people;

(ii) a member of the Council of Ministers, other than the Prime Minister, means the Prime Ministers; and

(iii) a member of Parliament, other than a Minister means the Council of states in the case of a member of that Council and the House of the people in the case of a member of that House;

(3) "Memorandum of complaints" means a memorandum of complaints alleging that a public functionary has committed any offence punishable under the prevention of corruption Act, 1988;

(4) "Inquiry" means every inquiry conducted under this Act by the Lokpal;

(5) "Lokpal" means the institution established under section 3;

(6) "Member" means a Member of the Lokpal;

(7) "Prescribed" means prescribed by rules made under this Act;

(8) "Public functionary" means a person who-

(i) Holds or has held the office of the Prime Minister. Minister, Minister of state or Deputy Minister of the Union; or

(ii) is or has been a member of either House of Parliament.

CHAPTER - II : MACHINARY FOR INQUIRIES

3. Establishment of Lokpal.

(1) As from the commencement of this Act, there shall be established, for the purpose of making inquires in respect of memorandum of complaints under this Act, an institution to be called the "Lokpal".

(2) The Lokpal shall consist of –

(i) A Chairperson who is or has been a chief justice or a judge of the Supreme Court; and

(ii) Two Members who are or have been the judge of the Supreme court or the chief justices of the High courts.

(3) The chairperson and every other member shall, before entering upon his office, make and subscribe before the president, or a person appointed in that behalf by the president, an oath or affirmation in the form set out in the Schedule.

4. Appointment of Chairperson and Members.

(1) The chairperson and member shall be appointed by the President by warrant under his hand and seal:

(2) Every appointment under sub-section (1) shall be made after obtaining the recommendations of a committee consisting of–

The Vice-President of India	Chairman;
The Prime Minister	-member;
The Speaker of the House of the People	-member;
The Minister in charge of the Ministry of Home affairs in the Government of India	-member;
The Minister in-charge of the Ministry of Law and justice in the Government of India	-member;
The Leader of the House other than the House in which the Prime Minister is a member of Parliament	-member;
The Leader of the Opposition in the house of the people	-member;
The leader of the Opposition in the council of States	-member;

Provided that in case, there is no ledger of opposition in the house of the people or the council of states, the leader of the single largest group or party in opposition to the government, as the case may be, in such House or council shall be deemed to be a member of the committee specified in clause (g) or clause (h), as the case may be:

Provide further that no sitting judge of the Supreme court or sitting Chief justice of a High court shall be appointed except after consultation with the chief justice of India.

(3) No appointment of a chairperson or a member shall be invalid merely by reason of any vacancy in the committee.

5. Chairperson and members to be ineligible to hold other office. The Chairperson or a member shall not be a member of parliament or a member of the legislature of any state or union territory and shall not hold any office of trust or profit (other than his office as the chairperson or a member) or be connected with any political party or carry on any business or practice any profession and accordingly, before he enters upon his office, a person appointed as the chairperson or a Member , as the case may be, shall, if –

- He is a member of parliament or of the legislature of any state or Union territory, resign such membership; or
- He holds any office of trust or profit, resign from such office, or
- He is connected with any political party , server his connection with it; or
- He is carrying on any business , server his connection (short of divesting himself of ownership) with the conduct and management of such business; or
- He is practicing any profession, cease to practice such profession.

6. Term of office and other conditions of service of chairperson and member.

(1) The chairperson and every other member shall hold office as such for a term of three years from the date

on which he enters upon his office or until he attains the age of seventy years, whichever is earlier:

Provided that he may -

(a) By writing under his hand addressed to the President, resign his office; or

(b) Be removed from his office in the manner provided in section 7.

(2) On ceasing to hold office , the chairperson and every other member shall be ineligible for -

(i) Reappointment in the Lokpal;

(ii) any diplomatic assignment, appointment as administrator of a Union territory and such other assignment or appointment which is required by law to be made by the president by warrant under his hand and seal; and

(iii) further employment to any other office of profit under the Government of India or the Government of a State

(3) The salary, allowances and other conditions of service of -

(i) the chairperson shall be the same as those of the Chief justice of India;

(ii) other members shall be the same as those of a judge of the Supreme court:

Provided that if the chairperson or a member is, at the time of his appointment, in receipt of a pension (other than a disability or would pension) in respect of any previous service under the government of India or under the government of a state, his salary in respect of service as the chairperson or, as the case may be, as a member, be reduced –

(i) By the amount of that pension; and

(ii) If he has, before such appointment, received, in lieu of a portion of the pension due to him in respect of such previous service, the commuted value thereof,

> *by the amount of that portion of the pension:*
>
> *Provided further that the salary, allowances and pension payable to, and other conditions of service of, the chairperson or a member shall not be varied to his disadvantage after his appointment.*

7. Removal of chairperson or member. The chairperson or a member shall not be removed from his office except by an order made by the president on the ground of proved misbehavior or incapacity after an enquiry made by a committee consisting of the Chief Justice of India and two other judges of the supreme court next to the chief justice in seniority, in which the chairperson or the member had been informed of the charges against him and given a reasonable opportunity of being heard in respect of those charges.

8. Member reason as chairperson or to discharge his.

(1) In the event of the occurrence of any vacancy in the office of the chairperson by reason of his death resignation or otherwise the president may by notification authorise the senior -most member to act as the chairperson until the appointment of a new chairperson to fill such vacancy.

(2) When the chairperson is unable to discharge his functions owing to absence on leave or otherwise the Senior most member available as the president may by notification authorise in this behalf shall discharge the functions of the chairperson until the date on which the chairperson resumes his duties.

9. Staff of Lokpal.

(1) The Lokpal shall for the purpose of assisting it in the discharge of its functions (including verification and inquiries in respect of memorandum of complaints) under this Act appoint of memorandum such other officer and employees as the President may determine from time to time in consultation with the Lokpal.

(2) Without prejudice to the provisions of sub- section (i) the Lokpal may for the purpose of dealing with any memorandum of complaints or any class of memorandum of complaints secure-

(i) the services of officer or employee or investigating agency of the central government or a state government with the concurrence of the Government, or

(ii) the services of any other person or Agency.

(3) The terms and conditions of service of the Officers and employees referred to in sub–section (1) and of the officers employees agencies and persons referred to in sub-section (2)(including such special conditions as may be considered necessary for enabling them to act without fear or favour in the discharge of their functions) shall be such as the president may determine from time to time in consultation the Lokpal.

(4) In the discharge of their functions under this act the officers and employees referred to in sub-section and the officer employees agencies and persons referred to on sub-section (2) shall be subject to the exclusive administrative control and direction of the Lokpal.

CHAPTER - III : JURISDICTION AND PROCEDURE IN RESPECT OF INQUIRIES

10. Jurisdiction of Lokpal

(1) Subject to the other provisions of this Act, the Lokpal shall enquire into any matter involved in, or arising from, or connected with, any allegation of corruption made in a memorandum of complaints:

Provided that the Lokpal shall not enquire into any matter involved in , or arising from, or connected with, any such allegation of corruption against the prime Minister in so far as it relates to national security, maintenance of public order, national defence and foreign relations:

Provided that Lokpal shall not inquire into any matter involved in, or arising from or connected with, any such allegation of corruption against any Member of either House of parliament unless the recommendation of the speaker of House of people or the chairmen of council of states, as the case may be, is received by it.

(2) The Lokpal may enquire into any Act or conduct of any person other than a public functionary in so far as it considers it necessary so to do for the purpose of its inquiry into any such allegation of corruption:

Provided that the Lokpal shall give such person a reasonable opportunity of being heard and to produce evidence in his defence.

(3) No matter in respect of which a memorandum of complaints may be made under this Act, shall be referred for inquiry under the commissions of inquiry Act, 1952.

11. Matters not subject to jurisdiction of Lokpal

(1) The Lokpal shall not inquire into any matter concerning any person if the Chairperson or any Member has any bias in respect of such matter or person and if any dispute arises in this behalf, the president shall, on an application made by the party aggrieved, obtain, in such manner as may be prescribed the opinion of the chief Justice of India and decide the dispute in conformity with such opinion.

(2) The Lokpal shall not inquire into any memorandum of complaints if the memorandum of complaints is made after the expiry of five years from the data on which the offence mentioned in such memorandum of complaints is alleged to have been committed.

12. Memorandum of Complaints.

(1) Any person other than a public servant may make a memorandum of complaints' under this Act to the Lokpal.

Provided that memorandum other a complaints in case of Prime Minister shall be made to the speaker of the house of people and the Lokpal shall consider only such memorandum of complaints as are referred to it by the speaker of the House of people:

Provided further that memorandum of complaints in case of minister of state or deputy minister of the union and member of either House of parliament shall be made to the Speaker of House of people or the chairman of council of states as the case may be and lokpal shall consider only such memorandum of complaints as are referred to it by the speaker of the house of people or the chairman of council of states as the case may be:

Explanation: For the purposes of this sub-section "Public servant" means–

- Any person who is a member of a defiance service or of a civil service of the union or a State or of an all India service or holds any post connected with defiance or any civil post under the union or a state;
- Any person in the service or pay of a local authority a corporation established by or under a Central provincial or State Act or a government company as defined in section 617 of the Companies Act 1956;
- Any person in the service of any other institution, concern or undertaking which is established by or under a Central, Provincial or State Act or which is controlled, or financed wholly or substantially by funds provided, directly by the Central Government or a State Government.

(2) The memorandum of complaints shall be in the presided form and shall set forth particulars or the offence alleged and shall be accompanied by such particulars and a corticated of deposit furnished under sub-section (3)or, if the complainant is under to make the deposit, an application for exemption from the

requirement as to such deposit .

(3) The complainant shall deposit such sum of money in such manner and with such authority or agency as may be prescribed and the certificate for such deposit shall be furnished in the prescribed form.

(4) Notwithstanding anything contained in the forgoing sub-section any letter written to the Lokpal by a person in any jail or other place for insane persons may if treated as a memorandum of complaints made in accordance with the provisions of this section.

(5) Notwithstanding anything obtained in the any other enactment, it shall be the duty of a police officer or other person in-charge of any jail or other place of custody or of any asylum or other place for insane persons to forward, without opening, any letter addressed to the Lokpal by a person imprisoned or detained in such jail place of custody asylum or other place to the Lokpal without delay.

13. Preliminary Scrutiny of Memorandum of Complaints by Lokpal.

(1) If the Lokpal is satisfied, after considering a memorandum of complaints and after making such verification as it deems appropriate that

(a) the memorandum of complaints is not made within a period of five years as specified in sub-section (2) of section 11; or

(b) the memorandum of complaints is manifestly false and vexatious;

The Lokpal shall dismiss the memorandum of complaints after recording its reasons therefore and communicate the same to the complainant and to the competent authority.

(2) The purpose for verification in respect of a memorandum of complaints under sub-section (1) shell be such as the Lokpal deems appropriate in the circumstances of the case and in particular, the Lokpal

may, if it deem it necessary so to do, call for the comments of the public functionary concerned.

14. Procedure in respect of inquiries

(1) If, after the consideration and verification under section 13 in respect of a memorandum of complaints, the Lokpal proposes to conduct any inquiry, it—

- Shall forthwith forward a copy of the memorandum of complaints to the competent authority;
- May make such orders as to the safe custody of documents relevant to the enquiry as it deems fit; and
- Shall at such time as it considers appropriate, forward a copy of the memorandum of complaints to the public functionary concerned as afford him an opportunity to represent his case.

(2) Every enquiry shall be conducted by the chairperson and the member sitting jointly and the place in which such inquiry is conducted shall be deemed to be an open court to which the public generally may have access so far as the same can continently contain them;

Provide that in exceptional circumstances and for reason to be recorded in writing, such inquiry may be conducted in camera.

(3) The Lokpal shall hold every such enquiry as expeditiously as possible and in any case complete the enquiry within a period of six months from the date of receipt of the memorandum of complaints;

Provided that the lokpal may, for reason to be recorded in writing. Complete the enquiry with in a further period of six months.

(4) Save as aforesaid the procedure for conducting any such enquiry shall be such as the lokpal considers appropriate in the circumstances of the case.

15. Evidence.

(1) subject to provisions of this section, for the purpose of any inquiry (including the verification under section 13), the lokpal–

(a) may require any public servant or any other person who in its opinion, is able to furnish information or produce document or relevant to such inquiry to furnish any such information or produce any such document; and

(b) shall have all the power of a civil court, under the court of civil procedure 1908, while trying a suit in respect of following matters, namely:-

- Summoning and enforcing the attendance of any person and examining him on oath;
- Requiring the discovery and production of any document;
- Receiving evidence on affidavits;
- Requisitioning any public record or copy thereof from any court or office;
- issuing commission for the examination of witnesses or documents;

  Provide that such commission, in case of a witness, shall be issued only where the witness, in the opinion of the lokpal, is not in a position to attend the proceeding before the lokpal; and
- such other matter as may prescribed.

(2) Any proceeding before the Lokpal shall be deemed to be judicial proceeding within the meaning of section 193 of the Indian penal code.

(3) No obligation to maintain secrecy or other restriction upon the disclosure of information obtained by or furnished to Government or any public servant whether imposed by any enactment or by any provision of low whatever, shall apply to the discloser

of information for the purpose of any inquiry (including the verification under section 13 under this Act.

(4) The government or any public servant shall not be entitled, in relation to any such enquiry or verification under section 13 to any such privilege in respect of the production of documents of the giving of evidence as is allowed by any enactment or by any provision of law whatever in legal proceedings.

Explanation: for the purpose of this section, "public servant" shall have the same meaning as is in section 21 of the Indian panel code.

16. Search and seizure.

(1) If the Lokpal has reason to believe that any document which, in its opinion, shall be useful for, or relevant to, any inquiry under this Act, are secreted in any place, it may authorize any officer any subordinate to it, or any officer of an investigating agency referred to in subsection (2) of section 9, to search for and to size such documents.

(2) If the Lokpal is satisfied that any document sized under sub section (1) would be evidence for the purpose of any inquiry under this act and that it would be necessary to retain the document in its custody, it may so retain the said document till the completion of such inquiry;

Provide that where any document is required to be returned, the same after retaining copies of such document duly authenticated thereof.

(3) The provisions of the code of criminal procedure, 1973 relating to searches shall, so far as may be, apply to searches under this section subject to the modification that sub-section (5) of section 165 of the said code shall have effect as if for the words "magistrate", wherever it occurs therein, the words "Lokpal" or "any officer authorized by it" were substituted.

17. Reports

(1) After the conclusion of inquiry, the Lokpal shall determine whether all or any of the offences alleged in the memorandum of complaints have or has been prove to its satisfaction and by report in writing shall communicate its findings to the complainant, the public functionary and the competent authority.

(2) The speaker, in the case of the Prime Minister or a Member of the people, and the chairman of the council of the states in the case of member of that council shall, as soon as may be, after the receipt of report under sub-section (1), cause the same to be laid before the House of the People of the Council of States, as the case may be while it is in session, and if the House of the people or the Council of states as the case may be, is not in session, within a period of one week from the reassembly of the said House or the Council, as the case may be.

(3) The competent authority shall examine the report forwarded to it under sub-section (1) and communicate to the Lokpal, within a period of ninety days from the date of receipt of the report, the action taken or proposed to be taken on the basis of the report.

(4) The Lokpal shall present annually to the president a consolidated report on the administration of this act and the president shall, as soon as may be after and in any case not later than ninety days from the receipt of such report, cause the same, together with an explanatory memorandum, to be laid before Each House of Parliament.

Explanation: In computing the period of ninety days referred to in this sub-section, any period during which parliament or, is not in session, shall be excluded.

CHAPTER - IV : MISCELLANEOUS

18. Expenditure on chairperson and members to be charged on the consolidated fund of India. The salaries, allowances and pension payable to, or respect of, the Chairperson and Members of the Lokpal, shall be expenditure charged on the Consolidated Fund of India.

19. Intentional insult or Interruptiôn to Lokpal

(1) Whoever intentionally offers any insult, or causes any interruption , to the Lokpal while the Lokpal or any of its Members is making any verification or conducting any inquiry under this Act, shall be punished with simple imprisonment for term which may extend to six months , or fine . or with

(2) The provisions of sub-section (2) of section 199 of the Code of Criminal procedure 1973, shall apply in relation to an offence referred to in sub-section (2) of the said section, subject to the modification that no memorandum of complaints in respect of such offence shall be made by the Public Prosecutor except with the previous sanction of the lokpal.

20. Power of Lokpal try certain offences

(1) When any such offence as described in sub-section (1) of section 19 is committed in the view or presence of the Lokpal may cause the offender to be detained in custody and may at any time on the same day take cognizance of the offence and after giving the offender a reasonable opportunity of showing cause why he should not be punished under this section, try such offender summarily, so far as may be, in accordance with the procedure specified for a term which may extend to one month, or with fine which may extend to five hundred rupees, or with both.

(2) In every case tried under this section, the Lokpal shall record the facts constituting the offence with the statement, if any made by the offender as well as the fining and the sentence.

(3) Any person convicted on a trial held under this section may appeal to the supreme Court.

(4) The Provisions of this section shall have effect notwithstanding anything contained in the Code of Criminal Procedure 1973.

21. Disposal of deposit under section 12 etc., and penalty for malafide memorandum of complaints.

(1) The sum deposited by a complainant in Pursuance of the provision of section 12 shall—

- In a case where the memorandum of complaints dismissed under sub-section (1) of section 13, stand forfeited to the Central Government
- If the Lokpal for reasons to be recorded in writing so directs, be utilized for compensating the public functionary comp lamed against, and
- In any other case be refunded to the complainant.

(2) If the Lokpal is satisfied that

- all or any of the allegation made in a memorandum of complainant have or has been substantiated either wholly or partly; and
- having regard to the expenses incurred by the complainant in reaction to the proceeding in react of such memorandum of complaints and all other relevant circumstances of the case the complainant deserves to be compensated or rewarded, the Lokpal shall determine the amount which shall be paid to the complainant by way of such compensation or reward and the lokpal shall determine the person by whom the said compensation or reward shall be paid after giving that person a reasonable opportunity of being heard.

(3) Every person who makes any memorandum of complaints which is held by the lokpal to be false and filed with malafide intention to harass the public functionary against whom such memorandum of complaints is filed shall be punishable as provided in Sub-section (4).

(4) When any offence under sub-section (3) is committed the lokpal may take cognizance of the offence and after giving the offender a reasonable opportunity of showing cause why he should not be punished for such offence try such offender summarily so far as may be in accordance with the procedure specified for summary that's under the Code of Criminal Procedure, 1973 and if such offender is found guilty of committing the offence sentence him to imprisonment for a term which shall not be less than one year but which may extend to three year and also to fine which may extend to fifty thousand rupees and may also award where fine to the public functionary against whom such false memorandum of complaints has been made such amount of compensation as the lokpal thinks fit.

22. Application of Act 2 of 1974. Notwithstanding anything contained in the Code of Criminal Procedure 197 and subject to the other provisions of this act any case pending before the Lokpal under sub-section (4) of section 21 shall any be transferred to another criminal court in accordance with the procedure contained in section 407 of that code and for the purposes of that section the lokpal shall be deemed to a court of session.

23. Conferment of additional function on Lokpal.

(1) The president may, by order in writing and subject to sub condition or limitations as may be specified in the order, require the Lokpal to inquire into any allegation (being an allegation in respect of which a memorandum of complaints may be made) specified in the provisions of section 13 the lokpal shall comply with such order.

(2) When the Lokpal is to make any inquiry under sub-section (1) the Lokpal N shall exercise the same powers and discharge the same functions as would in the case of any inquiry made on a memorandum of complaints under this act and the provisions of this act except section 21 shall apply accordingly

24. Person likely to be prejudicially affected to be heard. If any stage of the inquiry, the Lokpal

(a) considers it necessary to inquire into the conduct of any person: or

(b) is of opinion that the reputation of any person is likely to be prejudicially affected by the inquiry ;

The Lokpal shall give to the person a reasonable opportunity of being in the inquire and to Produce evidence in his deface'

Provided that nothing in this section shall apply where the credit of a withes is being impeached.

25. Protection of action taken in good faith.

(1) No suit prosecution or other legal proceedings shall lie against the Lokpal or against any officer employee agency or person referred to in section 9, in respect of anything which is in good faith done or Intended to be done under this Act.

(2) Save as otherwise provided in this act on proceedings or decision of the Lokpal shall be called in question in any court.

26. Power to Delegate. The Lokpal may by general or special order in writing and subject to such conditions and limitations in may be specified therein direct that any limitations as or duties imposed on it by or under this act {except the power under sub-section (1) of 12 the power to dismiss a memorandum of complaints under sub-section (1) of section 13 and the power under section 21} may also be exercised or discharged by the officers employees and agencies referred to in section 9, as be specified in the order.

27. Power to make rules.

(1) The President may, by notification in the Official Gazette, make rules for the purpose of carrying out the provisions of this Act.

(2) In particular, and without prejudice to the generality of the foregoing power, such rules may provide for—

(a) the manner in which the President shall obtain the opinion of the Chief Justice of India under sub-section (1) of section 11;

(b) the form of memorandum of complaints under sub-section (2) of section 12 and the fees, if any, to be accompanied therewith;

(c) the manner in which and the authorities of agencies with whom deposit shall be made under sub-section (3)of section 12 and the form in which certificate shall be furnished in respect of such deposits;

(d) the matters referred to in sub-clause (vi) of clause (b)of sub-section (1) of section 15; and

(e) any other matter which is to be or may be prescribed;

(3) Every rule made under this Act shall be laid as soon as may be after it is made before each house of Parliament while it is in session for a total period of thirty days while may be comprised in one sessions or in two or more successive session and if before the expiry of the session immediately following the sessions or the successive sessions aforesaid both houses agree in making any modification in the rule or both houses agree that the rule should not be made the rule shall thereafter have affected only in such modified form or be of no effect as the case may be so however that any such modification or annulment shall be without prejudice to the validity of anything previous done under that rule.

28. Removal of Doubts. For the removal of doubts it is hereby declared that nothing in this Act shall operate to confer or enable the conferring of any jurisdiction on the Lokpal to make any inquiry—

(a) into any allegation of corruption against or any act or conduct of—

- the president the vice-president, the speaker of the House of the People, the Deputy Speaker of the House of the People, Deputy Chairman of the Council of States;
- the Chief Justice or any other judge of the High Court or the Supreme Court;
- the Comptroller and Attorney General of India Chairman and other member of National Commission for Scheduled Castes and Scheduled tribes, the Chief Election Commissioner other Election Commissioner, the Chairman and other Members of the Union Public Service Commission or any other authority appointed under the Constitution of India; and

(b) upon its own knowledge or information.

29. Savings. Nothing contained in this Act shall be construed as affecting the consititution of, or the continuance of, functioning or exercise of powers by any Commission of Inquiry appointed under the Commissions of Inquiry Act, 1952 before the commencement of this act and no memorandum of complaints shall be made under this Act in respect of any matter referred for inquiry to such Commission before such commencement.

30. Amendment of Act 60 of 1952. In secction 3 of the Commisions of Inquiry Act, 1952, in sub-section (1), for the words "The appropriate Government may", the word, brackets and figures "Subject to the provisions of sub-section (3) of section (3) of section 10 of the Lockpal Act, 2007, the appropriate Government may" shall be substituted.

THE SCHEDULE
[See section 3(3)]

I, A.B .... having been appointed Chairperson for a Member) of the Lokpal co swear in the name of God/solemnly affirm that I will bear true faith and allegiance to the Constitution of India as by law established, that I will duly and faithfully and to the best of my ability, knowledge and judgement perform the duties of my office without fear or favour, affection or ill-will.

8

Protest for Arrest of Anna Hazare

Introduction

The Congress-led central government did everything to crush the agitation blocked all the roads leading to Jayaprakash Narayan Park, the epicentre of Anna's hunger strike, arrested Anna and his team members from their respective homes itself and tried to defame the agitation by making various false allegations people from all walks of life, filled the streets holding tiranga and shouting prominently two slogans Vande Mataram and Bharatmata ki Jai. "Now I could realise why these two slogans made the people die for the nation during the freedom struggle," said Rajesh Kochar, a second year student of Khalsa College while participating in the march at India Gate.

Wearing Gandhi caps, which had "I am Anna", the protesters came from diverse backgrounds and included a large number of youth, students, women, senior citizens, freedom fighters and even eunuchs. They carried the placards like 'Parliament is not supreme, People of India are supreme',

'We want corruption-free India', 'Uproot corruption or we will uproot this government', We respect Parliament, we hate Parliamentarians', 'Anna, we won't step back now, this corrupt government has to bow', 'Arrest of Anna is murder of democracy', 'Wake up Sonia-PM, you cannot make us fool', '15 August we gained freedom, 16 August we lost it', 'Anna wins, India wins', etc.

When the police reached Anna Hazare's residence at Supreme Enclave in Mayur Vihar to arrest him on August 16, people did not let it take Anna away. The policemen had to surmount a human wall of nearly 2 km drenched in a steady drizzle to accomplish their task. Wherever the police took Anna in the day, the crowd followed him. Before being arrested, Anna appealed to people to "keep the protest going as this is just the beginning". This arrest basically sparked off the protest of unprecedented magnitude across the country.

The most remarkable feature of this protest was its spontaneity. Although it was raining in Delhi since early morning, over 50,000 people reached Chhatrasal Stadium by afternoon. When the Stadium was full to its capacity and the police refused to arrest more protesters, they sat on the Ring Road and reverberated the atmosphere with slogans like Vande Mataram, Bharatmata ki Jai, Sarkari Lokpal dhokha hai abhi bacha lo mauka hai, Anna ko riha karo, varna sharm se doob maro, Anna nahin ye Aandhi hai, desh ka doosara Gandhi hai, Congress ki kya pehchan, bhrashtachar aur atyachar, Manmohan Singh jisaka tau hai, vo sarkar bikau hai, Sonia jisaki mammi hai, vo sarkar nikammi hai, Gali-gali mein shor hai, Sonia Gandhi chor hai, Bhrastachar mitega kab, janamanas jagega jab, etc.

Earlier in the morning, protesters, including former IPS officer Kiran Bedi and Shanti Bhushan, were brought to the Stadium after being detained from Rajghat and some other locations. It was followed by hundreds of buses full of protesters who smiled at the police but vent their anger on the Congress-led UPA government. They volunteered to go inside the Stadium despite the police ruling before noon that 'you can go in, but can't exit'. "The agitation will not stop. We will render full support to Anna Hazare till the Government agrees to constitute a strong Lokpal. Corruption has made our life miserable and we have to get rid of it at any cost now," said Kishore Chandra, a resident of Mukherjee Nagar who along with his neighbours was at the Stadium since morning. "I came here without informing my parents. So, I gave the police a wrong number so that they cannot call up my parents," said Anamika, a student of Delhi University while shouting slogans inside the Stadium. "An elderly person is fighting for the future of our children. Why should I not join him," asked Sunita Jain, a housewife from Gandhi Nagar.

Delhi Police had made full arrangement to stop people reaching Jayaprakash Narayan Park, Rajghat, Jantar Mantar and other possible places of protest. Over 5000 policemen were stationed at Bahadur Shah Zafar Marg alone. In the morning, the rain as well as the police did deter a few protesters, but the diehards tricked in two's and three's and gathered at Park from where they were detained. At Pragati Maidan, thousands of people gathered in the evening and marched down the road towards Supreme Court.

Over 20,000 people gathered outside Tihar Jail where Anna was detained. They took out a candle march in the evening and then remained standing there throughout the night. "I am not in a pub, mom. I am at Tihar," a teenage girl cried over her phone. Even the pesky mosquitoes couldn't take the sting out of people's enthusiastic slogans until morning when a fresh wave of Anna fans descended there. "I am here to support this great cause. Government must accept Anna's demands," said Surendra Gupta, a school teacher standing outside Tihar Jail. Shaken over the strong sentiments of people, the police, however, announced to release Anna at night of August 16 itself, but he refused to come out from the jail till he is granted unconditional permission for hunger strike.

The protest witnessed open support from Baba Ramdev's

Bharat Swabhiman Trust, Vishwa Hindu Parishad, Akhil Bharatiya Vidyarthi Parishad, Arya Samaj, RSS and hundreds of other organisations. But all had only one identity "I am Anna" and tiranga was their symbol. Baba Ramdev, on August 17, met the President of India requesting to accept the demands of Anna Hazare. Later, he went to Tihar Jail to meet Anna. Sri Sri Ravi Shankar Guruji also met Anna in Tihar the same day.

Till afternoon of August 16, Congress leaders tried their best to dismiss the agitation saying that a few thousand people did not represent the 'will' of the nation, but by evening the shaken government and the party were forced to admit that it was more than a mere numbers' game. It also alleged a 'foreign hand' behind the Anna campaign which only agitated the protesters further.

The protest on second day (August 17) was stronger than the previous day. Students boycotted classes, advocates did not attend the courts and people took leave from their offices. Seeing low attendance in the offices, the Union Home Minister P Chidambaram threatened the government employees with severe punishment if any of them joined the Anna agitation. The number of people in Chhatrasal Stadium doubled on second day.

In the evening, over 60,000 people assembled at India Gate and marched up to Jantar Mantar. The march choked the roads in and around India Gate, Janpath, Parliament Street and brought the traffic in Lutyen's Delhi to a halt. The sea of people was beyond one's imagination. Mothers joined the march with tiny children tugging on to their saris and duppatas, the elderly braving their creaking bones, students looking for a brighter future and professionals fed up with 'greasing palms to move government files'. Shouting slogans like Mein bhi Anna, tu bhi Anna, ab to sara desh hai Anna, Ye andar ki baat hai police hamare saath hai, Desh ke yuva sadakon par hain, tum kahan ho Rahul Gandhi? Vo sarkar nikammi hai jisame Rahul ki mammi hai, etc. People, especially the youth, coined their own slogans, wrote them on a simple paper and joined the march to be a part of the 'revolution'.

"Today I took half-day leave just to join this protest, as I didn't want to miss this historical revolution," said Dr Alka Tyagi, a lecturer of English literature in Dayal Singh College. Medical Students from Maulana Azad Medical College (MAMC) joined the protest in their uniform itself. "I came here directly from my class, as I feel the cure of corruption is must before completing the studies," said Pallava, a final year student of MAMC while carrying a placard displaying 'Cure for cancer-corruption: Anna, SOS'.

Though, Delhi Police refused permission of hunger strike to Anna Hazare, it allowed some Congress leaders to stage a dharna at Jantar Mantar demanding hanging of the killers of Rajiv Gandhi. When the protesters saw the Congress leaders staging this dharna, they irked and started shouting slogans against Congress leaders. The atmosphere became very tense, but immediately a group of Anna supporters formed a human wall to protect those Congress leaders. "We did it because we don't want our agitation to become violent at all," said an Anna supporter.

One more interesting feature of the agitation was that lakhs of people who could not reach Chhatrasal Stadium, Tihar Jail or India Gate, took out marches in the streets of their own colonies. There was hardly any colony in Delhi where such marches were not taken out. Similar reports were received from all parts of the country including the remote areas.

The agitation proved to be a jan andolan (mass movement) in the real sense, as in all the protest marches there was no identifiable leader and the self-disciplined public was the vanguard. One more fact is that lakhs of people carried tricolour in their hands but not a single incident of insulting the tricolour was reported from any part of the country. In fact, tiranga again proved to be the source of energy for the agitators. "Whenever we felt tired, we took up the tiranga in our hands and started shouting slogans. It not only refreshed us but also energised with renewed vigour to fight till the government bows down," said Avinash Gupta standing outside Tihar Jail since three days.

Till the time of going to press, Anna Hazare had reached Ramlila Grounds. He left Tihar Jail in a large procession on August 19 and reached Ramlila Maidan after paying tribute to Mahatma Gandhi at Rajghat.

Anna Hazare has united the nation against corruption. And cornered the Congress. The Manmohan-Sonia nautanki has been exposed with a deafening declaration that the people are the sovereign in a democratic polity. Is it the death knell for dynasty politics?

Fortunately, Anna has ignited a new sense of patriotism. The movement marked the assertion of an infectious brand of vitality, verve and élan. An assertive, demanding and incredible sense of national honour. Sixty five years after independence, the people of India have again seized the initiative. Again, Vande Matram and Bharat Mata Ki Jai have become fashionable. The battle cry of a resurgent India. On the vanguard is the youth. Anna has presented a promising national agenda.

This may not be India's Jasmine Revolt or August Revolution, but the nation in one voice has expressed its disapproval of the UPA trademark of loot and scoot. The people will no longer tolerate the disdain of the political class towards those who elect them.

The Congress, cleverly, with some support from other political parties, tried to pit the Parliament against the people's agitation. What we are witnessing in the streets of India is a rebellion against the tyranny of the elected representatives. The men and women whom the people have elected in good faith have started behaving as masters enjoying all privileges, power and pelf with a blind eye to the suffering of the voting class.

The demand for the Lokpal Bill is only symbolic of an aspiration for a truly democratic and benign social order. There is no point repeating the voluminous corruption charges against the rulers. It will not be an exaggeration to say that it has crossed all horizons of human imagination in this country.

Some say, corruption has become a way of life. That nobody is insulated from its scourge. When Anna started the movement early this year most people were skeptical about its success. Opposition parties had from time to time tried to organise agitations, dharnas and demonstrations against price rise and corruption without much impact. For almost a year, Baba Ramdev was going from village to village creating mass awareness against corruption. But the general feeling was that with the existing leadership in the political set up there was no chance for a large scale mass action. This made the ruling party brazen. The match was fixed and the game was to prove all are equally corrupt. The voters were presented with a fait accompli. You choose from the same basket of rotten apples or get lost. Everybody, knew that JP-moment had arrived, but there was no JP in sight. JP had propounded right to recall as an article of faith. An inseparable ingredient of a vibrant democracy. He had challenged the Emergency regime's arrogant claim that once elected "you huff and puff but suffer us for full five years". Of late, the establishment has perfected the system of sharing the booty with all in the circus. The people lost.

Anna has fitted into that vacuum. He is not after power, but to define the limits of power in democracy and remind our rulers that ultimately the veto is with the people. He emerged as the new messiah, the one whose word carried tremendous appeal. His detractors lost face. All actions and arguments proved counter productive. His charisma bridged all differences. And his biggest support came from the youth, and the class of people who are generally bracketed as indifferent, apolitical, perhaps even those non-voting section. That Anna was able to politicise all of them make them interested and concerned citizens in itself is a great achievement.

It is Anna's unblemished record of public service, his credibility that proved unassailable for the government. The Congress Party's ham-handed methods did not work against Anna. At every point, the government had to capitulate before Anna because his campaign is genuine, selfless and in public interest. He presented a new ray of hope for the people who had lost all faith in the political leadership. Equally, the mass simmering anger against corruption, black money and price rise had taken the lid off.

Politics, after all is about mass mobilisation, for a just and justifiable cause. In that sense, Anna has achieved a tremendous success, a spontaneous response and a well organised and disciplined campaign style.

What we are witnessing is nothing short of a revolution. Only on two earlier occasions in recent memory such grand scale people's participation was recorded. The first was under Loknayak Jayaprakash Narayan in mid-seventies. The second was during the Ayodhya movement, in the early nineties, propelled by L. K. Advani's historic Rath yatra. What makes these occasions historically defining, significant and arresting is the fact that at some level, both the movement and its protagonist have touched a raw nerve of the national psyche, offered a new idiom in public discourse and signaled a fresh beginning. The mirage may not last long. But as long as it lasts it's euphoric, transcending boundaries and barriers. Let the hangover of the past not make us wary.

Media Coverage

Anna sent to Tihar Jail, protests engulf India New Delhi, Aug 16, (IANS)

> *Civil society activist Anna Hazare was Tuesday arrested and sent to Tihar Jail as Delhi Police moved to stop his fast-unto-death to press for a strong anti-corruption Lokpal Bill, triggering swathes of unrest across the country and pitting the government against not just the opposition but also large sections of the public.*

Hazare, 74, was detained early Friday and later arrested and sent to prison to seven days judicial custody. His associates Arvind Kejriwal, Kiran Bedi and Shanti Bhushan were also detained with about 1,400 supporters all across the capital.

"Anna Hazare refused to sign a personal bond and has been sent to seven days judicial custody," Delhi Police spokesperson Rajan Bhagat told reporters, describing it as a preventive arrest.

The opposition went on the warpath to demand Hazare's release. As the Bharatiya Janata Party (BJP) said the move smacked of the excesses during Emergency and parliament was stalled, the outrage spread across the country, with reports of protests coming in from virtually every corner.

Hazare and Kejriwal were whisked away as they stepped out of an apartment in east Delhi on their way to the J.P. Park where police had clamped prohibitory orders and where the activists were planning to set the stage for their strike against the government's version of the bill that keeps the prime minister, judiciary and junior officials out of its ambit.

Hazare's supporters, who had gathered in hundreds in the apartment complex, shouted anti-government slogans and lauded the anti-corruption crusader who had gone on a hunger strike in April.

Just before his arrest, Hazare said in a recorded video message: "Don't let my arrest stop this movement. This is the nation's second struggle for freedom." As news of his arrest spread, thousands took to the streets in Delhi, denouncing the government and hailing Hazare. The biggest gathering took place at the Chattrashal Stadium in north Delhi. Major protests were also reported in Delhi University, outside the Tihar Jail, and on the street leading from Rajghat to J.P. Park.

Security forces had a tough time handling the crowds. Protests also gripped many states including Chhattisgarh, Uttar Pradesh, Himachal Pradesh, Maharashtra, Jammu and Kashmir, Madhya Pradesh and Orissa where people trooped out of their homes to voice their anger. Many shopkeepers downed shutters. In India's financial capital Mumbai, thousands gathered at various places.

"We are also requesting supporters to strike work tomorrow and support Annaji," a volunteer for India Against Corruption said. Celebrities too stepped in to verbalise their distress. Lyricist Javed Akhtar said: "I have had certain reservations about Anna's method but his arrest cannot be condoned. It is undemocratic, unacceptable."

The ripple effect was widespread.

"In a democracy, one has the right to protest in a peaceful manner. By detaining Hazare, the government is depriving the citizens of their constitutional rights," said P.K. Garg, a retired professor in Lucknow.

As the protests spread, the government attempted to clarify its position and said Delhi Police was not acting under political pressure and had made the detentions because Team Hazare had refused to agree to certain terms.

"If someone says we will defy the orders, I think this is unacceptable in a democracy," said Home Minister P. Chidambaram. "It is a real regret that police have taken this action."

The crisis for the government comes soon after the clampdown on a protest by yoga guru Ramdev on June 5. The opposition was quick to seize the opportunity.

BJP president Nitin Gadkari and the Communist Party of India-Marxist (CPI-M), neither of which agree fully with Hazare, called for demonstrations across the country Wednesday. "This government is bent upon crushing anyone who wants to protest against corruption," BJP spokesperson Ravi Shankar Prasad said.

The CPI-M said Hazare's detention and the police ban on his hunger strike showed how "the Congress leadership is intolerant to any anti-corruption movement as its government is steeped in high-level corruption".

The volatile situation was set to snowball further with protests planned through the day. Using SMS messages, twitter and television, Hazare supporters called for people to gather in protest.

Sensing Hour of R, Tihar Protesters Give War Cry

Durgesh Nandan Jha & Indrani Basu, TNN Aug 19, 2011, 05.36am IST

NEW DELHI: The government may have blinked on Anna Hazare's demands, but those protesting outside Tihar say the battle against corruption has just begun.

Hundreds of people continued to hold protests outside the Tihar Jail complex, India Gate and Chhatrasal Stadium. Their next stop is going to be the Ramlila Grounds on Friday, where Anna will continue his fast.

Hundreds of people who gathered at Jail Road say they feel compelled to carry on with the protests to keep the momentum going.

"I need to be here. How can I sit at home when I feel so strongly for something that affects each one of us? This is both for our present and our future generations. This is the time for action. And nothing can keep us from congregating here and spreading the message across. A fire burns inside me that doesn't allow me to stay at home. People are absolutely fed up with the government. Anna is the only ray of hope," said 72-year old VK Makkar.

People have also come up with unique ideas to give a fillip to the campaign. Each of one them stands up to narrate their own encounters with corrupt officials and politicians.

"I have done M.Phil from Delhi University and have also cleared UGC Net examination . I have appeared for several job interviews, but my candidature has been rejected. I was once told by an administrative official of a prominent university that I could get the job if I paid Rs 5 lakh. I could not pay and I am still unemployed," said Prahlad Shastri.

A housewife said she was shocked when a school

demanded a bribe for her child's nursery admission. In many cases, people claimed only those with the 'right connections' get jobs. Sharing their experiences made them stronger, they claimed.

One of the protestors said, "We find strength in our common travails. We will not tolerate this any more."

Protesters claimed if the Jan Lokpal bill proposed by Anna Hazare was accepted, it would induce fear among corrupt officials and politicians. "More than that, Anna's movement is a wakeup call for the youth to discourage corrupt acts," said Vikriti Gupta, a social activist .

Those at Tihar or India Gate included people from all walks of like schoolchildren, housewives, senior citizens and professionals. We are guided by our own conscience , a protester said. "Main bhi Anna, tu bhi Anna. Ab to saara desh hai Anna "was the dominant slogan almost everywhere.

"Anna has shown us the way. Now it is for us to carry forward this fight against corruption," said Rajinder Singh, 24, who claimed that he had been sitting outside the Tihar gate for two days.

Ramdev, Sri Sri Join Protesters at Tihar Jail

Press Trust of India

Posted on Aug 17, 2011 at 02:46pm IST

New Delhi: Yoga guru Baba Ramdev and the Art of Living Foundation head Sri Sri Ravishankar on Wednesday joined protestors expressing solidarity with Anna Hazare outside Tihar Jail.

Ramdev, with whom Hazare and his associates have differences due to his alleged links with Hindutva elements, reached Tihar Jail on Wednesday afternoon. He was denied entry in Tihar Jail to meet Anna Hazare.

Earlier, Ramdev submitted a memorandum against Hazare's arrest to President Pratibha Patil. Addressing protesters, Ramdev termed Hazare's arrest as a "conspiracy in the name of democracy".

"Anna is fighting for a strong Lokpal and his dream will be fulfilled. The whole country and all patriotic countrymen are with him in this struggle," he said.

Activists Kiran Bedi, Swami Agnivesh and Medha Patkar had earlier joined hundreds of protestors while a large number of the Gandhian's supporters took out marches across the city.

Anna Hazare: Anti-corruption Activist's Arrest Sparks Protests Across India

Thousands take to the streets after police detain Anna Hazare, who was due to begin hunger strike against graft

Jason Burke in Delhi

Guardian.co.uk, Tuesday 16 August 2011 14.06 BST

Tens of thousands of people took to the streets across India on Tuesday to protest against the arrest of country's most prominent anti-corruption campaigner and more than 1,000 of his followers.

Anna Hazare, a 74-year-old activist and one of India's most respected campaigners, was detained by police on Tuesday morning, hours before he was due to begin an indefinite hunger strike to demand tough new laws against graft. By evening about 1,300 of his supporters had been arrested in Delhi, local media said, and hastily organised demonstrations were underway across the country.

Opposition politicians accused Prime Minister Manmohan Singh's beleaguered administration, currently in the middle of its second term, of repeating draconian crackdowns of the 1970s or the actions of British former imperial rulers. "This is murder of democracy," said Arun Jaitley, a senior leader of the opposition Bharatiya Janata Party (BJP).

Singh's government has been on the defensive in recent months following a series of huge corruption scandals which, combined with rampant food inflation, have sparked public anger and sent poll ratings plummeting as well as rattling markets and foreign investors. The prime minister, 78, has been accused of being out of touch with public opinion.

Hazare's arrest caused public outrage, with protesters some wearing masks of Hazare or carrying banners bearing anti-corruption slogans demonstrating in western Punjab, eastern Orissa, the far south, northern Himachal Pradesh and elsewhere. In Ralegan Siddhi, Hazare's home village in central Maharashtra state, cattle were used to block traffic.

Sonia Nair, a 35-year-old housewife in the commercial capital of Mumbai said she had demonstrated by singing the national anthem in the centre of the city with hundreds of others. "It was much better than sitting in front of my TV being concerned and angry. I wanted to act. It is time to stand up in support of Anna rather than sit at home," Nair said.

In Hyderabad, Abdul Aziz Sheikh, a 26-year-old information technology engineer and activist, said he had been protesting all day and was organising a candle-lit vigil. "There has been no debate, no attempt to bring a consensus. This is totally unconstitutional," he said.

Santosh Hegde, the former Ombudsman for the southern State of Karnataka who made headlines last month by forcing the local chief minister to resign following corruption allegations, told local television channels that the government "wants to crush this movement".

Anger has been heightened by the detention of many other respected senior activists alongside Hazare. These include Kiran Bedi, one of India's first female police officers, widely respected for her own anti-corruption efforts. She tweeted from detention that she had refused an offer of bail.

Hazare's first hunger strike in April successfully forced the government to promise a parliamentary bill creating a special ombudsman with power to investigate and punish corrupt politicians, bureaucrats and judges. But the changes proposed by the legislation presented in early August were criticised by activists as insufficient. They accused the government of backtracking. Negotiations had been continuing over the activist's planned public "fast unto death" for several weeks.

Hazare had recorded a video to be released if he was arrested in which he called for a "second freedom struggle" in India, which threw off British rule in 1947. "Unless there is change, there is no freedom, there is no actual democracy, there is no true republic, there is no true people's rule. The protests should not stop. The time has come for no jail in the country to have a free space," he said in a message broadcast on YouTube following his detention. Both houses of parliament were adjourned after the opposition protested at the arrests.

Though politicians from all parties have been implicated in corruption scams, many figures associated with the biggest and most high profile cases of graft are from the ruling Congress party.

The biggest, which investigators believed involved senior figures from a main coalition ally of Congress, may have cost the country up to £25bn. Other charges focus on the high-profile Commonwealth Games in Delhi last year.

Opposition figures likened the crackdown on the campaigners to the 1975 "Emergency" when then-prime minister Indira Gandhi arrested thousands of opposition members to stay in power. Congress party officials and minister have stressed their duty to "uphold law and order".

Manish Tewari, a Congress party spokesman, said Hazare was surrounded by "armchair fascists, overground Maoists, closet anarchists". A crackdown earlier this year successfully broke up demonstrations by tens of thousands of followers of a fasting yoga guru protesting graft. Ritika Dutta, a 20-year-old political science student at Delhi University said she was shocked by the arrests. "This can only happen in India. People who are fighting against corruption are today behind bars with corrupt ministers.

An old-school social activist

Anna Hazare, whose real name is Kisan Baburao, is a former soldier with a long history of campaigning. He is an old-style Indian social activist evidenced by his spotless white clothes, the white cap, or topi, popularised by activists including Mohandas "Mahatma" Gandhi, and the pen in his top pocket as a marker of literacy. Hazare's vision of India is both deeply conservative and reforming.

A strictly teetotal Hindu, he has banned tobacco, meat and cable TV from the village where he lives and has campaigned against caste prejudice. Hazare also played a part in setting up India's revolutionary right to information laws. He does not have a mobile phone.

Earlier this year, his topi briefly became a sartorial icon with supporters wearing similar caps bearing the slogan "I am Anna Hazare" in English and Hindi. He is popular among the middle classes, the liberal elite and in the bigger cities.

Press Statement of CPI(M)
16 August 2011

The Polit Bureau of the Communist Party of India (Marxist) has issued the following statement:

Arrest of Anna Hazare Condemned

The Communist Party of India (Marxist) condemns the arrest of Anna Hazare and the ban on the hunger strike in Delhi. This is an attack on the democratic rights of citizens to protest peacefully. It shows how the Congress leadership is intolerant to any anti-corruption movement as their government is itself steeped in high-level corruption.

The Polit Bureau reiterates that the official Lok Pal Bill presented in parliament is weak and inadequate. A strong popular movement has to be built up to ensure that an effective legislation is adopted by parliament.

All Hands on Deck, But all at Aea

Diptosh Majumdar, TNN Aug 21, 2011, 06.35am IST

It's been worse than a comedy of errors. The midnight swoop at Ramlila Maidan was construed to be a resounding success administratively. The high-handed action may have invited widespread criticism but the government had achieved its goal: Ramdev was forced to leap from the rostrum and make a ridiculous effort to flee the spot in a borrowed salwar-kameez. That gave UPA-II the false confidence that authoritarian tactics sometimes do pay off in a democracy.

That swift victory the yoga guru's attempt to make an inglorious exit obviously could not win him much public sympathy at the Ramlila grounds also gave the UPA think tank the bright idea that they could arrest Anna Hazare and that his support base would automatically melt away. But wishes seldom gallop away like wild horses. From Tihar jail, Anna ruled. Surrounded by grovelling jailors, Anna called the shots. He was not going anywhere till he had his way. The Jan Lokpal bill must become a reality. The UPA-II was helplessly stranded ; its feet sinking into a quagmire of its own making.

Strange have been the tactics of the beleaguered government from the beginning of the anti-corruption movement. It was completely taken aback by the growing popularity of the Anna phenomenon during the first episode of the Jan Lokpal struggle earlier this year. After a degree of surrender to Team Anna, when it acquiesced and allowed the formation of the joint drafting committee, the government was already being accused by civil society of duplicitous dealing. The government, too, had suddenly found its voice, its spin doctors like Kapil Sibal and Salman Khursheed harping on the government position; dismissing the civil society draft as garbage.

The negotiations fell through while the joint drafting committee was deliberating the arguments of either side, and the government probably didn't realize that an adamant Anna with his inherent simplicity and Gandhian traits had been able to bond with the middle classes. There was a groundswell of support for him. The Manmohan Singh-led government had a lot of time before the monsoon session of Parliament began in early August to prepare a well-thought-out strategy of dealing with the 74-year-old activist. Anna had, after all, given the definite deadline of mid-August a long time ago. But, neither the government nor the Congress party had a gameplan to keep Team Anna in check.

Anti-graft Movement Turned into a Struggle for Democratic Rights

Deccan Herald

No one ever thought that a struggle for a strong Lokpal Bill would turn into a pitched battle for a right to protest.

It is interesting to observe that till yesterday, the man who was sought to be limited as merely an anti-graft crusader, changed overnight into a champion of democratic rights who is being compared to, among others, the Burmese Nobel peace prize winner Aung San Suu Kyi.

The metamorphosis of the anti-graft struggle to a democratic rights movement makes interesting reading, if one scrutinises the ups and downs leading to Anna's Hazare's arrest and release.

When the civil rights activist ended his fast at Jantar Mantar last April, none of his supporters thought he would have to return to the same spot with the same demand - a strong Lokpal Bill. The reason, India Against Corruption (IAC), the organisation which drafted a pro-people Jan Lokpal Bill and spearheaded the April agitation led by Anna, came out empty handed from the Joint Drafting Committee of civil society and the government.

By June end, Team Anna had to declare its intention of starting another phase of struggle. While ending his April fast,

Anna had warned the government that in the event of government failing to enact a strong Lokpal Bill by August 15, 2011, he would resume his fast from the very next day, August 16.

IAC applied on July 16 for police permission to launch the second round of indefinite fast by Anna, starting August 16. But the police was not ready to respond quickly to an application that had been submitted one month ahead of the proposed fast.

Finally, the police allowed Hazare to sit on a fast at Jantar Mantar, but not for more than a day as Parliament would be in session and a series of demonstrations were scheduled at the same venue. IAC was asked to suggest a different venue. When they opted to hold the protest at Ramlila Grounds, it was turned down on the same grounds.

There has been no precedence of denying permission for a fast at the chosen venue? Was it justified? Angry Kiran Bedi, Anna's supporter, fumes: "No! The decision was not at all administrative, it was political." She says that it has never happened in the country's history.

If we go by the war of words between the government and Team Anna during the drafting of the Lokpal Bill, it appears there must be truth in the allegation of Team Anna that the government was afraid of Anna's popular support and did not want him to repeat the performance.

The allegations of anti-graft activists gained further strength when the police permitted Narmada Bachao Andolan leader Medha Patkar to hold a sit-in-protest at Jantar Mantar, the very venue denied to Anna, to demand a "people friendly" land acquisition bill.

Police Agenda

Obviously, the police had two things on their agenda; first, it did not want to give Team Anna time to mobilise the people. Second, it must have intended to send them to a place not easily accessible to the people. So, the police decision was delayed till August 10.

Ultimately, both sides zeroed in on Jaiprakash Narain park near Rajghat. But, the Police immediately put 22 conditions, citing a Supreme Court ruling aimed at ensuring that no inconvenience is caused to general public by such activities.

Senior advocate and People's Union for Civil Liberties (PUCL) activist N D Pancholi has been an opponent of Anna's movement. But he too is critical of the Police saying, "Our Constitution has guaranteed the right to protest. Only condition is that it should be peaceful. If there is apprehension of violence, the police can deny permission. In this case, there was no possibility of violence."

And Anna's reply was natural. Like a true Gandhian, he appealed to the people to defy the police. Anna's subsequent arrest under the pretext of 'preventive detention' mobilised a public resistence as never before, with political parties rallying behind him though they have reservations about his version of Lokpal.

Government Cheated Me at Every Step: Anna

Express News Service

NEW DELHI: Sharpening his attack on the Centre, Lokpal crusader Anna Hazare on Sunday revealed how the government had cheated him at every step of his fight and warned of unparalleled protests across the country if the Bill was not agreed upon by August 30. Hazare was addressing thousands at the Ramlila Maidan, where his supporters had assembled after a 5-km march from the historic India Gate.

"The government's intention has never been noble and clean. They don't intend to stop corruption and that's why they put so many spokes in my effort to bring this Bill. After the Right To Information Act, the civil society has come together once again to put the corrupt behind the bars but the government ditched us," Hazare said. "There have been seven meetings in the last two months with five ministers. We put forth 71 points before them, but they backtracked," he added.

Narrating details of his arrest by Delhi Police on August 16, Hazare revealed how he had turned the tables on the officials. "The government tried to quash my protest by first agreeing to let me fast and later cheating me like they did to Baba Ramdev. At 5.30 am they came to call me, I agreed and went out with them. I was told later that I have been arrested. I was unfazed and said 'I am ready.' The cops were surprised. Then again in jail, they cheated. Then they wanted to send me out of the jail at the earliest but I refused until my demands were met," he said.

Hazare warned that if the government doesn't come to a decision by August 30, it will witness a mass movement across the country.

"I want people to make sacrifices without which nothing will move. Don't forget Bhagat Singh, Sukhdev and Rajguru. Sit in protest outside every minister's and MP's house. Sing bhajans of Raghupati Raghav Rajaram," he said.

JP Park in Delhi will be venue for govt-Hazare showdown
New Delhi, Aug 15, DHNS:

> *The UPA government and Anna Hazare are headed for a showdown after the Delhi Police denied permission for the anti-graft activist's indefinite fast starting here on Tuesday for a strong Lokpal.*

On a day when both sides hardened their respective stand, Hazare gave a call for a nationwide "go to jail agitation" in support of the anti-corruption watchdog, the police imposed Section 144 at the JP Park here prohibiting assembly of people.

Denouncing the police move, Hazare and his supporters declared they would march to the park and start their fast from 10 am on Tuesday. The Gandhian activist, who made a surprise visit to Rajghat, declared his resolve to launch his fast at the park. Hazare said he would continue his fast in jail if police arrest him. "If they release me, I will again come back to the park to hold fast. This will be repeated."

Hours after Prime Minister Manmohan Singh said in his address to the nation that the Lokpal bill was before Parliament, that everyone should wait for it and that 'corruption cannot be eradicated through holding of fasts', Hazare, in his 'parallel address to the nation', appealed the people to get arrested if the police take him away on Tuesday.

The Delhi police on Monday denied permission to Anna Hazare to sit on fast at the venue after Team Anna's refusal to accept restrictions like limiting number of days of fast to three days and number of protesters to 5,000. The denial came soon after the team submitted an undertaking to comply with only 16 of 22 conditions laid by the police.

The civil society fast plan gained support not just from the right-wing RSS and BJP, but also the Leftist CPM whose leader Brinda Karat said the right to protest cannot be questioned.

"The point here is one may not agree with the form of protest or with all the demands being raised by Hazare. However, his right to protest cannot be questioned. Saying once a bill is in Parliament there can be no protest in this country is highly undemocratic," she said.

Ban Justified

The government, however, justified the police action saying law of the land was equal for all and even political parties have to take permission for holding agitations.

"I do not want to say any harsh thing against anybody. The law of the land is equal for all. Be it the Congress, any other political party or any citizen, we all have to take the permission of the law and order machinery to carry out any protest or march," Information and Broadcasting Minister Ambika Soni told reporters here.

Replying to questions on Anna team's contention that its right to protest cannot be taken away, Soni said everybody has got a right to protest but permission has to be sought keeping in mind law and order and other factors. Soni dismissed allegation of civil rights activist Arvind Kejriwal that the police set the conditions on them at the behest of politicians saying any person making such allegation is "deliberately trying to mislead."

Asked whether they would approach court against the Delhi Police action, Kejriwal said: "All options are open and there is an option to go to court."

Bibliography

Balchand, K. (30 May 2011). "Contentious issues bog down Lokpal Bill panel". *The Hindu*. Retrieved 6 June 2011.

Basu, Durga Das (2003). *Shorter Constitution of India* (13th ed.). Nagpur: Wadhwa & Co. p. 1972. ISBN 978-81-8038-206-2.

Chauhan, Chetan (13 April 2011). "Anna Hazare has CEC Quraishi's vote for electoral reforms". *Hindustan Times*. Retrieved 24 April 2011.

Chavan, Prajakta (16 February 2011). "Practise existing laws first: Anna Hazare" (in English). Mumbai: The Hindustan Times. Retrieved 9 June 2011.

Chetan Bhagat (17 August 2011). "Anna Hazare's fight for change has inspired millions of Indians". Guardian, UK.

Damle, Manjiri Madhav (29 June 2004). "Trust funds used for Hazare's birthday: Jain". *The Times of India*. Retrieved 17 April 2011.

Datta-Ray, Sunanda (16 April 2011). "UNREAL REMEDIES – The best solution is to let existing systems start functioning again". Calcutta: The Telegraph. Retrieved June 2011.

Deshmukh, Vinita (12 September 2011). "The Village Roadshow". The Indian Express. Retrieved 8 April 2011.

Deshmukh, Vinita (7 April 2011). "Anna Hazare, our one, big hope, and why he can do it". Moneylife. Retrieved 8 April 2011.

Deshpande, Vinaya (29 March 2011). "Anna Hazare faults Lokpal Bill". *The Hindu* (Chennai, India). Retrieved 5 April 2011.

Dynamics of rural development:lessons from Ralegan Siddhi Publisher- Foundation for Research in Community Health, 2002. Original from The University of Michigan. Digitized 21 Jul 2009 Length 181 pages.

Engineer, Asghar Ali (1997-02-15). "Communalism and Communal Violence, 1996". *Economic and Political Weekly* **32** (7).

Florini, Ann. *The Right to Know: Transparency for an Open World*. New York: Columbia University Press. p. 24. ISBN 978-0-231-14158-1. Retrieved 2011-08-20.

Ghosh, Avijit (17 April 2011). "I was re-born in the battlefield of Khem Karan". *The Times of India*. Retrieved 17 April 2011.

Gosling, David L. (2001). *Religion and ecology in India and Southeast Asia*. London: Routledge. pp. 64–6. ISBN 0-415-24031-X. Retrieved 2011-08-20.

Govindu, Venu Madhav. "DEVELOPMENT WITH EQUITY" (in English). University of Maryland. Retrieved 2011-08-20.

Hazare, Anna (1997). *Ralegaon Siddhi: a veritable transformation*. Translated by B.S. Pendse. Ralegan Siddhi Pariwar Prakashan,. Retrieved 7 April 2011.

Hazare, Anna (in English). *My Village – My Sacred Land*. New Delhi: CAPART.

Hazare, Anna; Ganesh Pangare, Vasudha Lokur (1996). *Adarsh Gaon Yojana: government participitation in a peoples program : ideal village project of the Government of Maharashtra*. Hind Swaraj Trust. p. 95. Retrieved 2011-08-20.

IANS (1 Jun 2009). "Plot to kill Magsaysay winner Anna Hazare revealed" (in English). Mumbai: IBM Live – A Time Warner Company. Retrieved 12 June 2011.

Ismail Serageldin, David R. Steeds (1998). *Rural well-being from vision to action*. World Bank Publications. p. 433.

Jim Yardley (August 20,2011). "Antigraft Activists in India Intensify Drive for Reform". The New York Times.

Jim Yardly (August 21, 2011). "Thousands Back Antigraft Hunger Strike in New Delhi". New York Times.

Joshi, Poornima; Kavita Chowdhury and Sangeeth Sebastian Kurien (17 April 2011). "Congress continues to target Anna Hazare on Narendra Modi remark". India Today. Retrieved 11 June 2011.

Joshi, Sandeep (7 April 2011). "Support pours in for Hazare's movement". *The Hindu* (Chennai, India).

Kohari, Alizeh (16 August 2011). "Hunger strikes: What can they achieve?". *BBC News*.

Kumar, Vinay (9 Jun 2009). "Lok Sabha told of Padmsinh Patil's arrest" (in English). New Delhi: The Hindu. Retrieved 4 June 2011.

Lakshmi, Rama (9 April 2011). "India agrees to protesters' demand on graft panel". *The Washington Post* (Bangalore). Retrieved 9 April 2011.

Malviya, Alok (30 July 2011). "Lawyers hold protest in Allahabad in support of Anna Hazare" (in English). Allahabad: Lawetal news.. Retrieved 30 July 2011.

Marothia, Dinesh K. (2002). *Institutionalizing Common Pool Resources*. New Delhi: Concept Publishing. pp. 122=8. ISBN 81-7022-981-2. Retrieved 2011-08-20.

Marpakwar, Prafulla (28 April 1999). "Snap polls woke Rane up to sack Gholap". *Indian Express*. Retrieved 10 April 2011.

Marpakwar, Prafulla (29 Jul 2010). "State all set to scrap MAT" (in English). Mumbai: The Times of India. Retrieved 9 June 2011.

Nangia, Pankaj (19 August 2011). "Anna Hazare leaves jail to begin public hunger strike". *The Guardian* (London).

Naqshbandi, Aurangzeb; Chatterji, Saubhadra; Sharma, Nagendar (16 August 2011). "Refusing to leave jail, Anna holds government hostage". *Hindustan Times*. India. Retrieved 17 August 2011.

Parsai, Gargi (28 July 2011). "Hazare to go on fast from August 16 demanding revised Bill" (in English). New Delhi: The Hindu. Retrieved 30 July 2011.

Periwinkle Environmental Education Part-X Author-Harendra Chakhaiyar, Publisher- Jeevandeep Prakashan Pvt Ltd, ISBN-8177444948, 9788177444940

Poddar, Ganeshdatta (2009) (in English). *Globalization, liberalization, and environmentalism*. Rawat Publications. pp. 262 pages. ISBN 8131601099, 9788131601099. Retrieved 19 July 2011.

Press Trust Of India (14 October 2009). "HC rejects Padamsinh Patil's bail plea in Hazare's complaint" (in English). Mumbai: The Hindustan Times. Retrieved 10 June 2011.

Press Trust Of India (26 September 2009). "Anna Hazare files police complaint against Padamsingh" (in English). Mumbai: The Hindu. Retrieved 10 June 2011.

PTI (16 December 2009). "Padamsinh gets bail in Anna Hazare murder plot case" (in English). Aurangabad: Zee News. Retrieved 12 June 2011.

PTI (30 July 2011). "Lokpal: VHP calls for support to Hazare" (in English). Mumbai: The Economic Times. Retrieved 30 July 2011.

Radhika Ramaseshan. "Hazare runs into civil society protest". The Telegraph.

Raghuvanshi, C. S. (1995). *Management and Organisation of Irrigation System*. New Delhi: Atlantic. p. 44. ISBN 81-7156-560-3. Retrieved 2011-08-20.

Ralegan Siddhi Authors: Ramesh Awasthi, Dashrath K. Panmand, Foundation for Research in Community Health (Bombay, India) Publisher: Foundation for Research in Community Health, 1994. Original from The University of Michigan. Digitized 22 Dec 2009. Length 92 pages

Raman, Anuradha; Smruti Koppikar (18 April 2011). "Wielding The Broom"*: Outlook.*

Rao, Shashank (28 July 2011). "Taxi union to join Hazare's fight for lokpal" (in English). *Hindustan Times* (Mumbai). Retrieved 30 July 2011.

Reilly, Carmel (2007). *Ralegan Siddhi: a special community*. Thomson Nelson. pp. 24 pages.

Roberts, Alasdair. *Blacked Out: Government Secrecy in the Information Age*. Cambridge University Press. p. 3. ISBN 9780521858700. Retrieved 2011-08-20.

Seabrook, Jeremy (1986). *Victims of development: resistance and alternatives*. Verso. p. 250.

Seabrook, Jeremy (1993). "Regenerating the Countryside" (in English). *Victims of development: resistance and alternatives*. Verso. p. 250. ISBN 0860913856,. OCLC 9780860913856. Retrieved 14 June 2011.

Seabrook, Jeremy. *Victims of Development: Resistance and Alternatives*. London: Verso. pp. 109–17. ISBN 0-86091-385-6. Retrieved 2011-08-20.

Sharma, Kalpana (8 April 2011). "Anna Hazare: India's pioneering social activist". Mumbai: BBC. Retrieved 9 April 2011.

Sharma, Nagendar (4 June 2011). "Keeping PM out of Lokpal breach of UN law: Team Anna". *Hindustan Times*. Retrieved 6 June 2011.

Sharma, Reeta (20 January 2001). "Anna Hazare: A fearless crusader". The Tribune. Retrieved 9 April 2011.

Singh, Abhimanyu (17 April 2011). "Anna's next target is electoral reform". *The Sunday Guardian*. Retrieved 24 April 2011.

Sivanand, Mohan (1986). *Why God Saved Anna Hazare*. The Reader's Digest Association. Retrieved August 2011.

Sivanand, Mohan (1986). *Why God Saved Anna Hazare*. The Reader's Digest Association, Inc. p. 3. Retrieved 4 August 2011.

Tare, Kiran (30 Mar 2010). "Liquor to ooze from chikoo, jambhul" (in English). Mumbai: DNA. Retrieved 11 June 2011.

TNN (15 Oct 2009). "Hazare plaint: Court rejects Padamsinh's bail plea" (in English). Mumbai: The Times of India. Retrieved 12 June 2011.

Trishna Satpathy,, Aasha Kapur Mehta (September 2008) (in English). *Escaping poverty: the Ralegan Siddhi case*. Hyderabad: Chronic Poverty Research Centre of Indian Institute of Public Administration (IIPA). ISSN 978-1-906433-20-8. Retrieved 14 June 2011.

Yardley, Jim (18 August 2011). "Unlikely Echo of Gandhi Inspires Indians to Act". *The New York Times*. Retrieved 19 August 2011.

Index

R

S

T

V

W